CHINESE
BRUSH PAINTING

CHINESE
BRUSH PAINTING

PAULINE CHERRETT

THE WELLFLEET PRESS
WELLFLEET

A QUINTET BOOK

Published by Wellfleet Press
10 Enterprise Avenue
Secaucus, New Jersey 07094

This edition produced for sale in the U.S.A.,
its territories and dependencies only.

ISBN 1-55521-723-0

This book was designed and produced by
Quintet Publishing Limited
6 Blundell Street
London N7 9BH

Creative Director: **Terry Jeavons**
Designer: **Wayne Blades**
Project Editor: **Sarah Buckley**
Editor: **Jenny Millington**

Typeset in Great Britain by
Central Southern Typesetters, Eastbourne
Manufactured in Hong Kong by
Chroma Graphics (Overseas) Pte. Ltd. Singapore
Printed in Hong Kong by
Leefung-Asco Printers Limited

CONTENTS

INTRODUCTION

Chinese Brush Painting is an art form that has gained a tremendous amount of popularity in recent years. Its apparent simplicity and the oriental spirit behind this fascinating subject appeal to many who wish to explore traditional techniques. The use of familiar materials, paper, brush, ink and water to capture the essence and spirit of the subject can transform the artist's ideas, and in many cases change the techniques and attitudes even of established artists. Pablo Picasso was greatly influenced by Chinese brushwork as can be seen in some of his bullfighting pictures where simple strokes show all the ceremony and tension involved.

Chinese Brush Painting has been practised for hundreds of years and the styles have changed enormously over time, giving a rich and varied tradition. The earliest painting in China was as decoration rather than representational illustration and there was great freedom in the interpretation of subjects from life. New influences were introduced as people from other countries came to China, and since it was also a very large country, varying styles evolved in both the north and south.

Silk was painted from 400 BC, and paper from AD 105. Other surfaces included bone and shells (for early calligraphy or pictograms), pottery and wood. As emperors and governments changed, so the fashion for freestyle or meticulous painting and calligraphy appeared.

Philosophy and symbolism play a large part in Chinese art. The equipment used and the subjects chosen often have beautiful names and descriptions. Paintings were often done as gifts and so suitable subjects would carry a hidden message. Studios and workplaces would be set out with care, each 'treasure' in the ideal place for maximum visual effect. The beauty and classical lines of an object would be discussed and appreciated at length with colleagues and fellow artists. Once the surroundings were right, the artist or scholar could start work. Often, groups of *literati* painters would gather in ideal and inspiring scenery, discuss what was in front of them and produce poems and paintings together.

RIGHT **Part of a large traditional figure painting scroll by Zhu Zhen Sheng showing a scholar and his servant (carrying an instrument). The inscription says 'Wang Ziyou planted ten thousand bamboos which make the River Wei so beautiful. Under the moonlight the swaying bamboo casts a shadow on the window and brings the autumn sounds to the ears. My old friend is so elegant and open-hearted'.**

LEFT **The contrast in style and technique between the previous picture and these blackcurrants shows how much room there is for personal style to develop.**

The subject was examined in a visual way, thought about, and only much later committed to a painting or poem. Very often, the artist left the scene and returned to the studio to carry out the work. In this way the Chinese have always expressed far more of their inner feelings about a subject, rather than giving an exact representation.

The traditional Chinese way of learning to paint was to copy 'the Masters'. An artist would have an apprentice who ground ink, mixed colours and unrolled paper, and it would be quite a time before he would be allowed to put brush to paper. He was expected to observe closely all that the Master did, as there was very little verbal

RIGHT **Ti flowers, painted by the author with a variety of brush loadings, illustrate a simple method of expression within Chinese Brush Painting. Varying the brush loading and the directions that the flowers face adds liveliness and interest.**

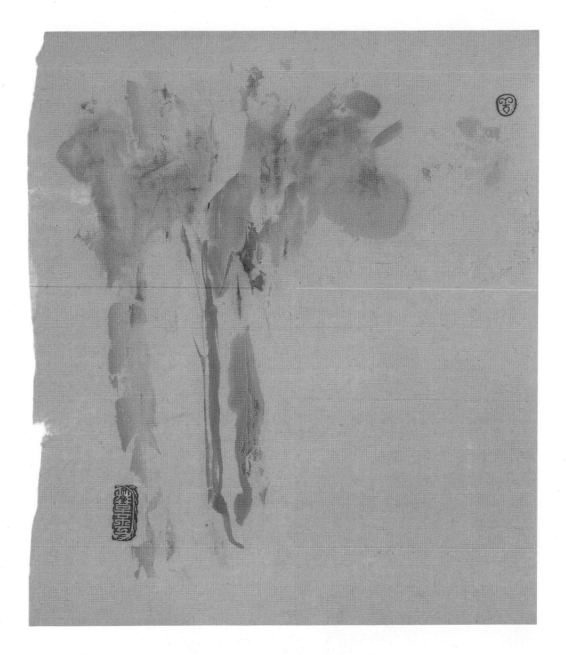

These trees were painted using the wrinkle technique. Different colours and blends of colour can be introduced. Although it is best to keep the composition simple.

instruction. The first subjects that the apprentice painted were always copies of other paintings and sometimes a Master would put his own seal (or *chop*) onto a student's work to indicate approval. This makes it difficult to attribute paintings.

In a Chinese Brush Painting, the space around the subject is as important as the brush-strokes. That space should always add something to the painting. In a complex landscape for example, it may be that the spaces are part of the image rather than merely the background.

The term, 'Chinese Brush Painting' is used because the techniques and brushstrokes require that only Chinese style brushes are used. The way brushes are made creates air spaces and it is these air layers that hold an unusual amount of water/ ink/colour. A lot of effort is saved by using an appropriate brush.

The Chinese style of painting alerts the artist not only to the outer appearance of a subject, taking in structure, texture and behaviour, but also to its inner spirit and essence.

MATERIALS AND EQUIPMENT

The equipment required for Chinese Brush Painting falls into two categories. The first is essential equipment, the second includes many items which are often pleasing to look at and to use but which are not essential to the art.

As usual, the Chinese have a beautiful description for the main equipment – the Four Treasures or the Four Gems. These are brush, paper, inkstone and ink stick. As with most art equipment there are varying qualities and grades. An artist should select the best items within the budget available – bearing in mind that there are cheaper, plain versions and also those with a more pleasing appearance. The choice is purely personal, provided a reasonable standard is obtained.

BELOW It is a Chinese man, Meng Tien, who is credited with the invention of the brush and therefore it is not surprising that the best quality brushes are Chinese. For this reason I recommend that all brushes be Chinese, except *Hake* brushes which may be Japanese. Brushes can be purchased in all sizes; singly or in boxed sets like these.

Some of the equipment can be purchased in art shops but take care that the ink and brushes are not Japanese (these are not as suitable as the Chinese versions). If classes are available the tutor will often have equipment for sale or loan. There are mail order suppliers and of course some Chinese shops stock painting materials. Expert advice can be hard to come by, however, as it is rare to find a supplier who also paints.

BRUSHES

The correct brush is very important. If used with care a wide variety of strokes and effects can be achieved. Choose the right brush and it will do the work for you! According to the ancient Chinese you had to have ink and brush before you could paint – this may seem to be self-explanatory, but what they meant was that you had to have ink tones and shading with the brushstrokes, outline and modelling strokes with the shades of ink. Some artists enjoy using the point of the brush for outline strokes or meticulous work, whilst others like to use the whole of the brush in a looser style. The brush is used to record the shape, attitude and texture of the subject and should be a 'slave of the artist'.

Meng Tien is credited with the invention of the first brush in the third century BC although it is thought that some brushstrokes were used on pottery as long ago as 4000 BC. The best brushes were highly valued and even buried in special tombs. The art of brush making was exported from China to Japan between 618 and 906 and there are still some similarities between ancient brushes and those made today.

There is no substitute for a traditional Chinese brush. The way in which it is made gives it extreme flexibility and a great capacity for holding liquid. These are the qualities needed to form most of the strokes. There are 18 different kinds of lines and 30 different kinds of dots. Chinese calligraphy consists of lines and dots, and a picture is often described as being 'written'.

Brushes are made from a variety of materials, all natural. In the past, they have been made of anything from feathers to human-hair but the list available now in the West is perhaps less exotic! Rabbit-, wolf-, weasel-, and horse-hair are all brown-hair brushes, and in the order listed gradually get stiffer and more resilient. These are used for a variety of strokes. Sheep-, and goat-hair are white-fibre brushes and are much softer. Brushes made from pig bristle are white and very stiff. The soft brushes are less resilient and more pliant.

When painting a landscape, dry brushstrokes are required together with highly textured effects. Horse-hair brushes are well-suited to this and will also give gnarled branches for an old pine tree. To paint bamboo or orchids, it is a matter of choice between brown-hair brushes which may well be called 'plum blossom', 'orchid' or 'bamboo', or one of the softer white brushes made from sheep- or goat-hair. Chinese artists, especially those trained in northern China, use the white brushes for many purposes. A soft hair brush can lead to more interesting strokes, although it is harder to control. Artists influenced by southern China, Singapore and Malaysia use wolf- or brown-hair brushes to a far greater extent. Some artists have only one or two brushes, others have every conceivable variety.

Brushes are also made from combinations of hair. These use the best features of each hair, for example white outside and brown inside, which provides softness and the ability to hold more liquid, with the centre giving a better point. There are many combinations, but you need to know the properties of each particular hair to realize the full potential of the brush. For washes, *hake* brushes are used, either the Chinese or the Japanese varieties. There are also cheap Chinese brushes like panpipes, (several brushes joined together), which can be used for this purpose. To produce an even wash you will need more than one brush, but they need not be exactly the same. The width of these brushes will depend upon the size of your paintings, but it is possible to work in small areas so there is no need to buy bigger brushes just for one painting that happens to be larger than usual.

Chinese artists often give their brushes fanciful names – 'coincident moon' (romantic

meetings associated with 7th July), 'smokey cloud', 'keep the best point', 'crane' or 'giraffe neck', 'red pine' and 'white goose'.

The length of the brush varies a great deal. The longer the hairs or fibres the more flexible the brush will be, but practice is needed to control the longer brushes. In the beginning, the artist will tend to use most of the brush, but as skill is improved

ABOVE **The fibre for soft brushes is mainly sheep- or goat-hair (pictured here) and will be useful for soft strokes such as petals or leaves. The brushes vary in length and roundness – the choice will depend on the scale of your painting.**

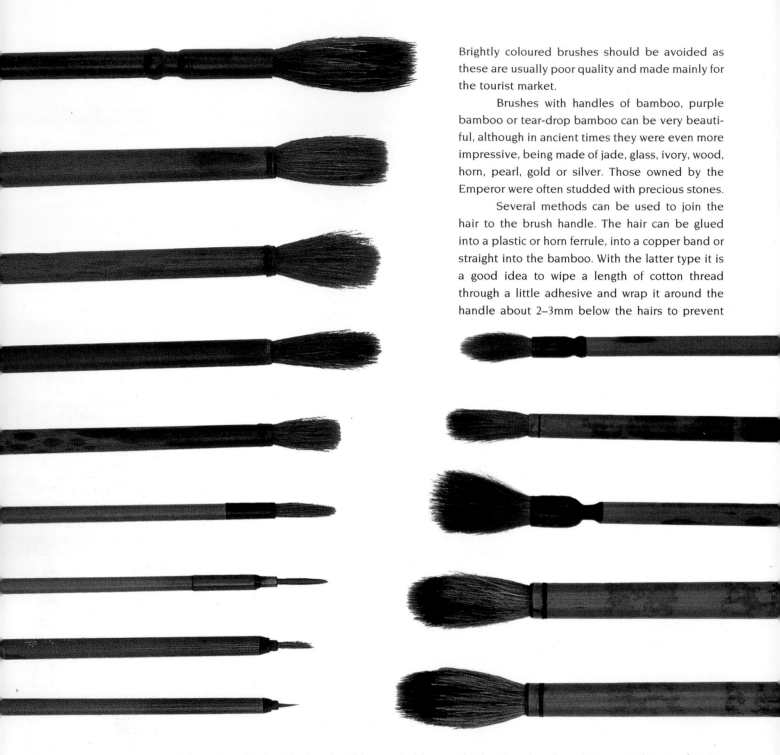

Brightly coloured brushes should be avoided as these are usually poor quality and made mainly for the tourist market.

Brushes with handles of bamboo, purple bamboo or tear-drop bamboo can be very beautiful, although in ancient times they were even more impressive, being made of jade, glass, ivory, wood, horn, pearl, gold or silver. Those owned by the Emperor were often studded with precious stones.

Several methods can be used to join the hair to the brush handle. The hair can be glued into a plastic or horn ferrule, into a copper band or straight into the bamboo. With the latter type it is a good idea to wipe a length of cotton thread through a little adhesive and wrap it around the handle about 2–3mm below the hairs to prevent

ABOVE **Firm and flexible brushes giving a good point are usually wolf-hair or similar. Again the size and quantity of these brushes will depend on the artist's choice of style and scale.**

only up to two thirds of the brush will be used with the rest held 'in reserve'. It is better to use a brush that is too large rather than one that is too small, although more control is needed. There are some very short brushes available, often in souvenir sets, called rose brushes which indicates their primary use, but for many other purposes they are too short.

the bamboo handle splitting. As Chinese glue can dissolve in hot water, brushes should always be washed out in cold or lukewarm water. The brush and handle must be dried in a towel or tissue and laid horizontally to dry. Dry brushes may be stored upright in a brush pot or hung upside down on a brush hanger. Never leave brushes standing in a

OPPOSITE PAGE

RIGHT **Mixed hair brushes such as leopard and wolf, sheep and wolf or rabbit and weasel, are more difficult to obtain. These brushes are perhaps better for the more advanced painter who will be able to make maximum use of the inherent qualities of the different fibres.**

LEFT **Stiff brushes are used for figures and landscapes. The hair is often from horse or pig. A light touch will add plenty of interest to strokes from these brushes and the pressure applied should be varied to add contrast.**

BELOW **For Chinese Brush Painters the brush is the means by which noble thoughts are translated onto paper, and as such should be carefully cleaned and stored. New brushes are protected by an alum solution to make a stiff point. This must be washed out before use. The bamboo or plastic covers shown on the left must be discarded.**

water pot; when not in use they should be supported on a brush rest.

When brushes are new, they are very pointed and stiff. This is due to a protective coating, on the hairs usually alum, which must be removed with luke-warm water before use. The size of the brush is difficult to assess before the alum solution is washed away. The bamboo or plastic cap must be discarded; trying to replace it will damage the brush. For protection when carrying the brushes around it is best to use a split bamboo brush-roll or a flexible table mat.

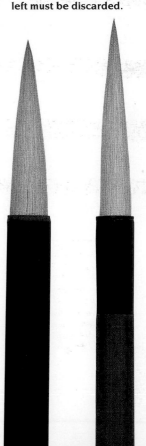

PAPER

Paper has been in use since at least AD 105, and possibly as early as 95 BC. Some modern papers are still very similar to those first ones. Because paper was so highly regarded emperors had special buildings as paper stores.

In the East there are many varieties of paper available but there is a much smaller choice in the West. Paper can be bought in sheets (flat pack or rolled together), continuous rolls, or large sheets which have been folded. Some artists have extra large sheets made for them, others join several sheets together when making a scroll.

Always try to choose the best paper for the scheme in hand. There are two ways of deciding . One is to use practice paper before moving on to the better version. The other approach is to use the better paper straight away. As there are different papers for different subjects, try out as many types as possible. You should soon find out which best suits your style of painting and which you feel most comfortable with. The examples in this book are carried out on many different papers.

One of the problems with all paper is that the batches can vary dramatically. One batch will be excellent for a favourite subject, but the next could prove unsuitable (or perhaps even better!). The ideal is to become accustomed to as many variations as possible.

Sometimes other papers such as mulberry and bamboo are available. These are more expensive, and therefore it is preferable to have some idea of their best use. The bamboo paper is a dark cream colour, and has a pleasant texture. Because it is so expensive it is often used for smaller paintings, mainly landscapes. The mulberry paper is much whiter with a more even texture and longer fibres than many other handmade papers. Dry brushstrokes in ink or colour executed on this paper are full of expression. Window papers, which as the name suggests was used instead of glass, (often from Korea) can also be used, but these are usually brought in by individuals from abroad. Many other types of paper are available in the East under a wide variety of names.

Paper is available in a wide range of absorbencies, giving different effects, for example where a fluffy animal is painted, or where a wet landscape is required. Any absorbent paper will give an effect, whether it is practice or handmade paper, but some will be better than others for a specific task. It is useful to make notes and attach a sample of the paper if you really wish to make the most of the different types.

When paper is out on the work surface, take care not to splash or mark it. When grinding the ink, place your hand along the side of the ink stone to prevent drops of ink falling onto the sheet which is ready to use. It is best to roll up any spare paper and put it out of harm's way.

SILK

Before the introduction of paper, silk was used as the base for paintings. It is still sometimes used today but rarely, as it is expensive. If plain silk is available it will need sizing with alum if it is to be used for watercolour paintings. It is possible to buy properly prepared painting silk, either on its own or backed with paper. This comes in a limited range of colours, ranging from cream to old gold. Its absorbency will vary depending on the preparation, but in general it is similar to meticulous paper.

It often seems that silk and paper from the past has discoloured over the intervening years, but the brown colouration is usually due to a coating of anti-insect solution applied over the finished painting. To imitate this effect, strong cold tea can be used as a wash.

INK STONE

The freshness of ink is of the utmost importance. Grinding the ink with due regard to the purpose for which it will be used is said to produce better work. The process of grinding the ink also prepares the mind and the wrist of the painter for the first brushstroke. A time for beautiful thoughts! Although liquid ink is used by contemporary artists, it must be fresh, and is used mainly to save time.

An ink stone must be capable of producing fine ink without damaging the brush. In the past these were handed down from generation to generation, and were therefore prized possessions. In T. C. Lai's *The Four Treasures*, ink stones are said to date back to the year 596.

There are several designs of ink stones from simple rectangular or circular student stones to

THE FOUR MAIN TYPES OF PAPER

Moon Palace or practice paper. This is from Taiwan or Japan and is machine made. It is very white with one smooth side and although very cheap and useful as practice paper, it is bland and without character. It can be purchased in rolls 300mm (12"), 450mm (18") and 600mm (24") wide or in A3 sheets. It is classed as semi-absorbent.

The second type can also be classed as practice paper and is usually made of grass- (*mao bian*) or wood-pulp. Again it has one very smooth side but is a pleasing yellow colour. Some Korean and Yuan shu papers also come within this colour range. They are not quite so absorbent and are available as sheets.

The Yuan shu paper is more difficult to mount than other types.

The third type is Xuan paper. This is hand made and a lovely creamy colour. It comes in different absorbencies and varying thicknesses; single, double and triple thicknesses give different effects. Some of this paper has more 'blemishes' in it than other types. The most common version is unsized.

The last paper is sized (meticulous) Xuan. This is usually thick and is not so easily obtainable. Any line painted on this variety does not spread into the paper. You can buy this paper as single large sheets, or in a roll of 10 sheets 1800mm (6') long.

BELOW Various papers are shown with the same brushstrokes. An effort was made to apply the same pressure and use the same amount of ink in the brush for all examples.

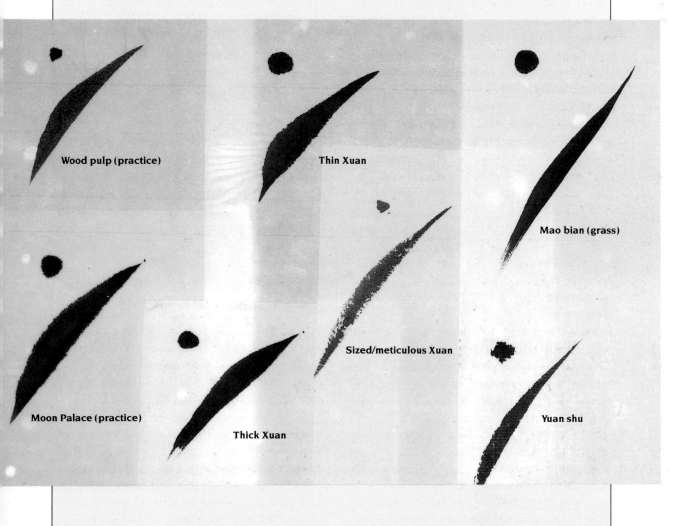

Wood pulp (practice)

Thin Xuan

Mao bian (grass)

Moon Palace (practice)

Thick Xuan

Sized/meticulous Xuan

Yuan shu

ABOVE An ink stone must be capable of producing fine ink without damaging the brush. In the past these were handed down from generation to generation, and were therefore prized possessions. Ink sticks were often equally prized, being previously made of jade or pearls. Again ink sticks vary in size, shape and quality. The bottled ink with the orchid on the label is good quality and often used. All liquid ink must be carefully washed from brushes.

ornate and carved antiques. Between these two extremes are many shapes, sizes and degrees of decoration. Ink stones are often carved from river slate or various stones giving many subtle colours. In the past, they were also made from jade and ceramics. The latter were often in shades of turquoise or green.

The grinding surface is usually circular or rectangular, and smooth to the touch. The stone must be impermeable and the smoothness of the stone will dictate the fineness of the ink. Some stones come with a lid of the same material, others are enclosed in a wooden box. The lid helps to prevent the ink from drying out. With a good stone you should not be able to hear the ink being ground.

However, a stone can be too smooth. In this case the ink will take too long to grind and will lack structure. This can happen with cheaper versions made from moulded slate dust set in resin. This can easily be detected if you look on the base of the stone and see ripples where the resin has contracted on setting. (Do not confuse this with tooling marks which are regular lines.) Although these moulded stones are satisfactory to begin with, after a short period of use they become extremely smooth and will no longer grind the ink. They are very black in colour.

INK STICK

Ink sticks are often beautifully decorated and many are collected purely for their appearance. In the past they contained ground jade or pearls, and sticks from a particular maker were especially prized. Their value was given as ten times that of gold! The first known ink was made in the year 221 when pine soot was mixed with lacquer.

An ink stick with a sheen or a matt finish should be chosen, rather than a glossy one and the weight of the stick should be light for its size. There are several different colours – blue-black, brown-black and a true black, depending on the part of the pine tree that has been used.

The sticks are made from pine- or oil-soot and resin, and it is the quantity of resin that makes the sticks so variable. Take care that the stick is not left in contact with a wet ink stone – the resin will adhere to the stone so severely that the stone may be damaged on separation. Get into the habit of drying the end of the stick on a piece of tissue if you find that it starts to crack. You should store an ink stick in the dark, in a cool place. The resin tends to deteriorate in time and an old ink stick may well crack and flake. If it is fresh the stick will have a pleasant smell, often of sandalwood or pine.

When grinding the ink, make enough for your painting but not too much so that it is left to dry. The ink stick should be used from one end only, with the stick held vertically, rather than sloping. Do not use more water than you need; to make thick, black ink takes 200 revolutions for a teaspoonful of water!

When the ink is being ground you should have some idea of the purpose for which it will eventually be used; whether it needs to be very black, or light grey, dry or wet. There are five main descriptions of the colours – burnt ink, thick ink, dry light ink, light ink and wet ink. (The circular seal inscription is 'Five kinds of colour'.) Mixing any two or three of these together will create differing effects on the paper and the study of all the combinations could last a lifetime.

Bottles of liquid ink are also available. This varies enormously in quality, and some varieties are poor. Ink should be fresh and the age of that sold in this country is hard to establish. With the poorer kinds it is difficult to obtain subtle shades by dilution. It is also very important that the liquid ink is washed out of the brush properly. It is possible to pour liquid ink onto an ink stone and grind an ink stick into it to obtain a thicker black, but liquid ink is difficult to use if a very dry black is required. For some techniques the ink can be left overnight to dry and will then granulate when mixed with water.

ABOVE **Impression from a bronze seal saying 'Five kinds of colour'.**

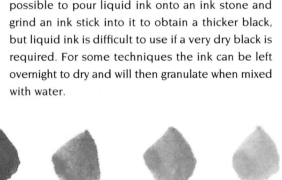

LEFT **By varying the dilution of the ink, seven recognized shades are possible.**

LEFT **Five 'colours' of ink. The seal can be used when the ink effects on the paper are considered to be good. It is common to see two or three of the colours in a painting, not all five together.**

| Burnt ink | Thick ink | Light ink | Dry, light ink | Water ink |

COLOURS

(also called paints and pigments)

Chinese paintings are often carried out solely in shades of black giving a monochrome effect. Adding a red seal is called 'adding an eye to a dragon'. However, many artists enjoy using colour, and in Chinese painting this involves natural materials (although some substitutes are now used). In landscapes and some early styles the colour is used very lightly and sparingly, with the ink giving the structure of the painting. Some of the modern free-style painting shows a much brighter and more dominant use of colour where the structure of the subject is formed by coloured pigments. There is little point however in using too much pigment as this will cause problems when mounting the work.

BELOW From right to left – Teppachi colours in porcelain pans, Chinese granules which are packed in small neat boxes and Chinese tube colours. Also shown are a typical chrysanthemum palette and Western stacking dishes, used for mixing colours.

properly. Although some of the traditional Chinese colours are very hard to obtain, coloured inks should not be used for Chinese painting techniques.

The Eastern paints which are sold in this country vary in quality, as do the Western versions. If buying a set of tubes you should look for Chinese Painting Colours. However, if in doubt, use the price of the paint as an indication of quality – in the case of Chinese paints, it's a reliable method. White gouache may be used sparingly for highlights to eyes etc. It is sometimes used, again for highlighting, in the Lingnan style of painting.

Flake colours are obtainable in some Chinese shops and by mail order. These are small pieces of colour; bright red, rough red, dark red, indigo, sky blue, burnt sienna, vermilion, peony,

Chinese Brush Painting is basically a watercolour technique, exploiting the transparency and translucency of the paints which are obtained from mineral or vegetable sources. Western watercolours can be used, although they tend to contain additives and some colours do not soak into the paper

crimson – the last two being the most expensive. There is also rattan yellow, made from a poisonous plant, and this is in a solid block over which you wipe your brush to obtain the colour. The flakes can be placed in small dishes, either a Chinese version (like a small, handleless cup), or a set of

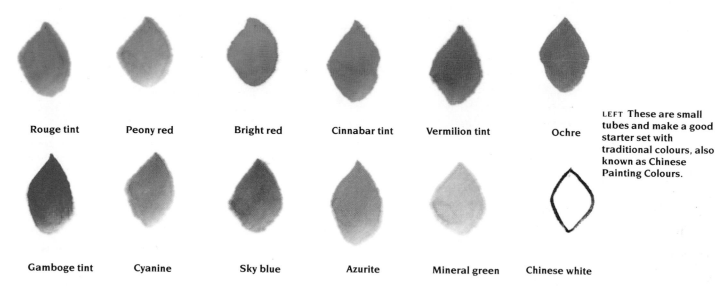

Rouge tint   Peony red   Bright red   Cinnabar tint   Vermilion tint   Ochre

Gamboge tint   Cyanine   Sky blue   Azurite   Mineral green   Chinese white

LEFT These are small tubes and make a good starter set with traditional colours, also known as Chinese Painting Colours.

stacking dishes that many Western artists will already have. To release the colour quickly pour warm water onto the flakes.

Other Chinese mineral pigments come in powder form which has to be mixed with gum, and is therefore not so popular. The most convenient way to obtain these beautiful stone greens and blues is to buy tubes.

Japanese colours in porcelain dishes are another alternative. There are fourteen colours which differ slightly from their Chinese counterparts, but are a good substitute and convenient to use.

To darken or make a colour less bright, black is often added, usually black ink. Sometimes however a particular pigment will react with the ink and granulation will occur. This can be avoided by using black paint instead but it will give a more matt appearance. Black should never be added to flower colours, nor should white be added to leaf and branch colours.

Coloured ink sticks are available in sets. These are mainly used for calligraphy and as each colour requires a different ink stone, are less practical for painting.

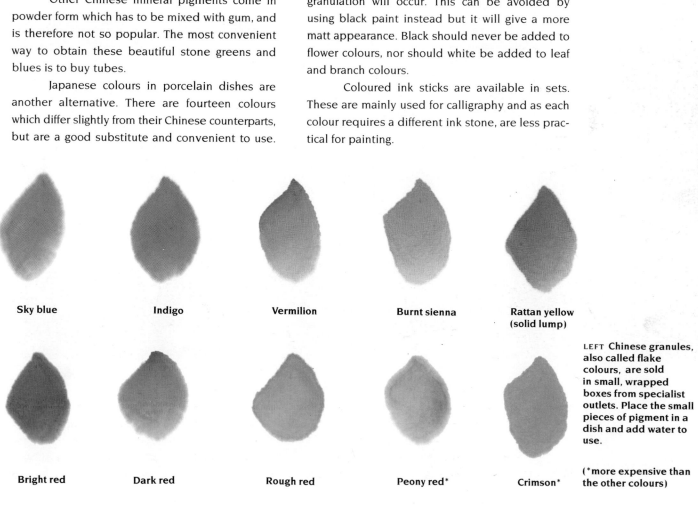

Sky blue   Indigo   Vermilion   Burnt sienna   Rattan yellow (solid lump)

Bright red   Dark red   Rough red   Peony red*   Crimson*

LEFT Chinese granules, also called flake colours, are sold in small, wrapped boxes from specialist outlets. Place the small pieces of pigment in a dish and add water to use.

(*more expensive than the other colours)

RIGHT **There are 14 Japanese *Teppachi* colours sold in porcelain dishes. Whilst these are not necessarily traditional Chinese colours they are easy to use and readily available.**

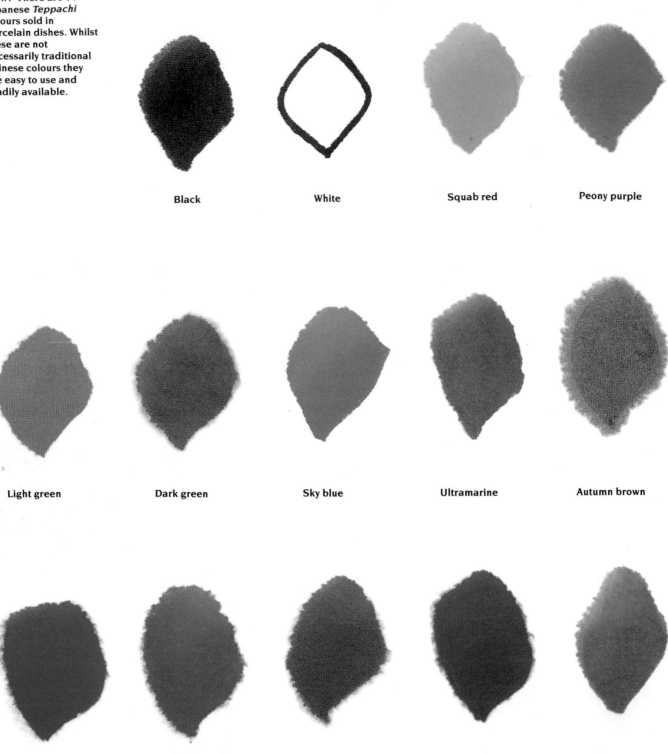

Black   **White**   **Squab red**   **Peony purple**

Light green   **Dark green**   **Sky blue**   **Ultramarine**   **Autumn brown**

Brillian yellow   **Cloeseed yellow**   **Burnt sienna**   **Vermilion**   **Bloody red**

WATER POTS

These can be anything from a yoghurt pot or jam jar to an ornate porcelain container. It is best to use two pots so that you always have clean water on hand. A small salt spoon or something similar can be used with the water pot to ladle water onto the ink stone. Ink sticks should not be dipped into the water pot as they will crack.

made from many materials – wood, stone, metal or porcelain. The designs are often traditional, featuring mountains, dragons and bamboo. The hangers and brush pots are used for storing the brushes when not in use. The pots are usually ceramic or wood, but sometimes metal. Again bamboo is a favourite for material and for decoration. The hangers are invariably wooden.

LEFT **All the equipment traditionally used in the past, including the pots and water droppers shown here, formed part of the 'scholar's desk'. Some were simple and cheap, others were of great value. Today these items are collected, both by artists and non-painters alike.**

PALETTE

There are several traditional patterns of palette. Some are called chrysanthemum dishes, others incorporate a similar design with a Ying and Yang water pot. Whilst these are very pleasant to use, a Western palette or a plain white plate can be just as good, although on a flat plate the colours may tend to flow together. If using a larger amount of ink or colour, as a wash for example, then the plate will be useful. Another option if larger quantities of liquid are required is to use a plain fondue plate which will have much larger segments. Department stores are a good source for these.

OTHER ACCESSORIES

BRUSH RESTS, BRUSH POTS AND HANGERS

Brush rests are used during painting so that the wet brushes do not roll around the table and spoil either the painting or any spare paper. They are

LEFT **Two designs of wooden brush hanger. The lefthand version can hold six to ten brushes and takes up minimum room on the table. The righthand type is in the form of a 'dragon pine tree' and holds ten brushes of varying length.**

TOP These brush pots of various sizes, together with brush rests (for use during painting) form part of the 'scholar's desk' and are not always recognized as such.

ABOVE Seals can be made from stone, bronze, ivory, horn and jade and may incorporate either a signature of the artist or a studio name, or a poem or saying. Artists who are also seal engravers often recarve their seals after grinding off the previous inscription.

OPPOSITE PAGES A third design of brush hanger will take 16 to 20 brushes. Extra long brushes can be hung from the ends. The brush pot is used for standing brushes in, but they must be dried horizontally before placing in the brush pot.

PAPERWEIGHTS

The paper needs to be held firmly in place while you are working although this does not mean that the paper cannot be moved during painting. Any form of weight can be used from coins and curtain weights to brass or inlaid wooden slats.

PAINTING FELT

This is the best surface to paint on although it can be difficult to find in the West. A well washed and felted woollen blanket is a good substitute. When applying a wash on a painting the blanket is perhaps even better than the felt. The cheapest alternative is newspaper. If you find the ink is spreading too much, try changing to a more absorbent newspaper or a piece of blanket.

SEALS

In order to sign your work in Chinese style you may like to have your own seal or *chop* carved. These are dealt with in more detail in Chapter 12.

STARTING OUT

Before starting to paint you need to think about what is ahead. With expensive Western watercolour paper, you will have to consider the expense, but with Chinese paper the cost is much less and you should not feel the same restriction.

A Chinese Brush Painting is built up from lines and dots, put together in such a way as to form a shape or design which has meaning and creates an impression. A painting is therefore often described as being written. The artist aims to paint a picture which will convey the structure, habit and likeness of the subject with life and feeling. This is described by the Chinese as having *chi* or spirit. Without this the painting will be dull and lifeless.

You will be faced with a sheet of white paper and must 'manage' the black marks that you put on it. A Chinese painting must not be crowded. In order to learn, the Chinese copy 'the Masters'. We in the West need to do this to an even greater extent, because we have not been exposed to their culture from birth, and have not absorbed the Eastern concepts of space and expression. Even Chinese artists need to learn the rules, study them, learn to use them expressively and eventually break them in order to progress.

The paintings may look simple however, strokes must be learnt and skills accumulated to produce the effects to order. The skill lies in controlling the amount of liquid in the brush, the pressure applied to the paper, and the effects produced. The right equipment will help you achieve this. A good quality brush and the correct brush for the purpose is essential. A palette and ink stone with a well-defined edge to wipe the brush against will make it easier to control the amount of ink or fluid in the brush. A light touch and sensitive approach will assist in keeping the correct pressure. Co-ordination will come naturally to some people but must be learnt by others.

RIGHT Assemble your equipment and lay out the table to start. You should ensure that you have good lighting conditions, room to paint freely and a seat of adequate height.

Your purpose is to encourage the paper to absorb the ink, or colour in the manner that you intend. There should be no spare pigment on the surface, therefore the way the colours are blended and mixed is most important.

THE FIRST STAGE

Before you start work, find a comfortable place to paint. You may be lucky enough to have the space to permanently leave your equipment out ready to use. You may have to clear away to prepare your table for meals, or pack the equipment into a bag to take with you to classes.

You will need a level surface large enough to hold your equipment and the paper ready for painting. For blending the colours, choosing the ink tones etc, you should work in good light using either daylight or artificial light. Another important factor is the correct working height of both chair and table. When you are seated ready to work, you should be able to move your arm, bent at right angles at the elbow, across the table without the elbow brushing the worksurface. Then you will have the free arm movement you need.

Having decided on your working space, set out the equipment. You will save time and accidental spillage by setting the area out in the same way each time. The paper should be placed in front of you, with weights to hold it in place. The ink stone should be to your right (all these instructions are for a right-handed person, reverse them if you are left-handed), along with brush rest, brushes (with the stiffness soaked out), ink stick, water pots, colours and palette. This ensures that you are not continually reaching across the paper to load brushes and risking ink or paint dropping onto the painting. Protect the paper with your hand while grinding the ink as an extra precaution.

Now you are ready to begin. Start by grinding the ink stick, trying to achieve dark, thick ink. You do not need to press hard, but try to keep the movement even and rhythmic. You should be thinking about what you are going to paint, trying to visualize it in your own mind, even if you are making a copy. It is said that you should be thinking noble thoughts in order to prepare yourself. Having ground the ink, load your brush with water. As with a woollen sweater that you put into a bowl to wash, the hair or fibre of the brush may not take up the water immediately. Wipe the brush carefully on the side of the pot and then load your brush with ink.

The loading of the brush is of the utmost importance and can make the difference between control and chaos. If your pot or palette has a well-defined edge you could use it to wipe out all the excess water. As you load ink (or paint) onto the wet brush, some of the ink will merge with the water, thus making the colour in the heel of the brush lighter than in the tip.

The way you hold the brush is also important. Try to hold it like a chopstick. Start by placing the brush between the second and third fingers, with the handle against the nail of the third finger. Support that finger with the little one and use the index finger to support the second finger. Place the tip of the thumb on the handle forming a cavity in the palm of your hand which could hold something like an egg. Do not grip the brush too hard and start off by holding the brush about halfway up the handle. You will gradually find yourself getting used to this hold, and will naturally move your

LEFT **When you are ready to start, add water to the ink stone with a salt spoon, dropper or brush. As you become more accustomed to this style of painting you will find several additional items amongst household equipment which may be of use.**

LEFT **When grinding the ink, protect your painting and steady the stone with your other hand. Try to grind with a steady, fluid motion. To achieve this try to relax and empty the mind of cares and worries, thinking instead of the painting you are about to start.**

LEFT **When the ink is of the desired consistency, wipe the brush on the ink stone or palette to release some of the ink/colour and to adjust the amount of liquid within the brush.**

hand up the brush if making larger strokes, and down the brush for detail. Your strokes will have more freedom if you hold the brush correctly – if you have trouble remembering try writing letters etc, using your pen in this way.

You should paint with a free arm, try not to rest on the table. If you are painting detail and need to rest, support just your wrist, not the side of your hand otherwise the strokes will be stilted.

When painting soft strokes such as petals or leaves, the brush should be slanting, for stems or branches it should be held upright. Try to think of the strokes as soft or powerful and adjust the angle accordingly. For a soft stroke the tip of the brush will be to one side of the stroke, for a powerful or strong stroke the tip will be the main part of the brush in contact with the paper. The more pressure you apply to the brush, the broader the stroke.

RIGHT Any powerful stroke or one which needs strength requires the brush to be held in an upright position. An upright brush and additional pressure at the start is required for stems etc.

FAR RIGHT For soft petal shapes however, you will need to use an oblique brush angle. This will be required in both vertical and horizontal directions. The wrist and grip on the brush therefore must be used flexibly enough to allow circular movement.

RIGHT In order for the hand/wrist to be able to move the brush in all directions, the arm must be held away from the table and be free from support.

Using the palette and some water, dilute the ink to get as many shades of grey as possible. Chinese ink is considered capable of dilution into seven separate shades, black plus six different greys. Practise putting these shades onto the paper. Try to control the amount of liquid in the brush to prevent the strokes from running.

Because lines are painted in different ways, you should know the effect you wish to create before putting brush to paper. For a fine line, wipe the brush well on the palette, hold the brush upright, touch the paper very lightly and move quickly. For a thick, wet line, you can still hold the brush upright, but allow more liquid in the brush and move more slowly. More liquid will flow from the brush onto the paper and give a thicker line, the outline will also be less distinct and sharp.

Experiment by placing various parts of the brush onto the paper: the point will give one effect,

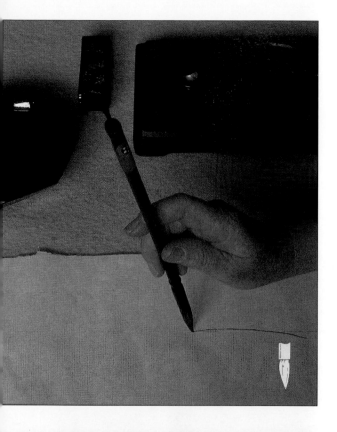

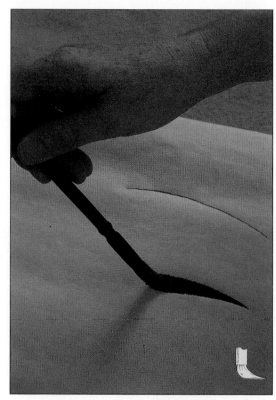

FAR LEFT How the brush is held is of vital importance to the success of the painting and strokes. With the brush held like a chopstick, use a light pressure with an upright brush to achieve a fine line.

LEFT Pushing the brush while applying increasing pressure will give a thin start to the stroke, followed by a line which gradually thickens. How quickly this happens will depend on the amount of pressure applied.

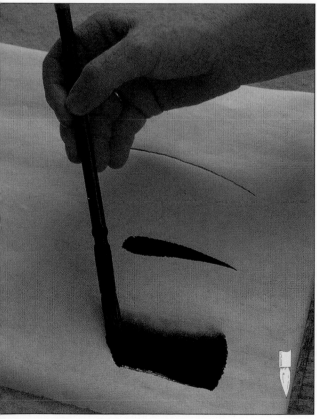

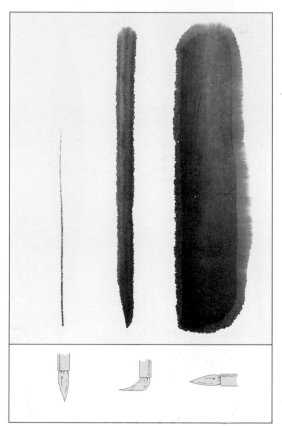

FAR LEFT Use the side of the brush to achieve a wide stroke. All of the brush may be used, but it is best to leave some 'in reserve'.

LEFT Different marks can be made on the painting depending on the pressure, loading and part of the brush that is in contact with the paper. The three symbols denote, from left to right, an upright brush, an upright brush applied with pressure and an oblique brush.

Strokes are shown
varying in thickness
and with differing start
and finish techniques.
The brush is lifted and
lowered to give the
desired effect.

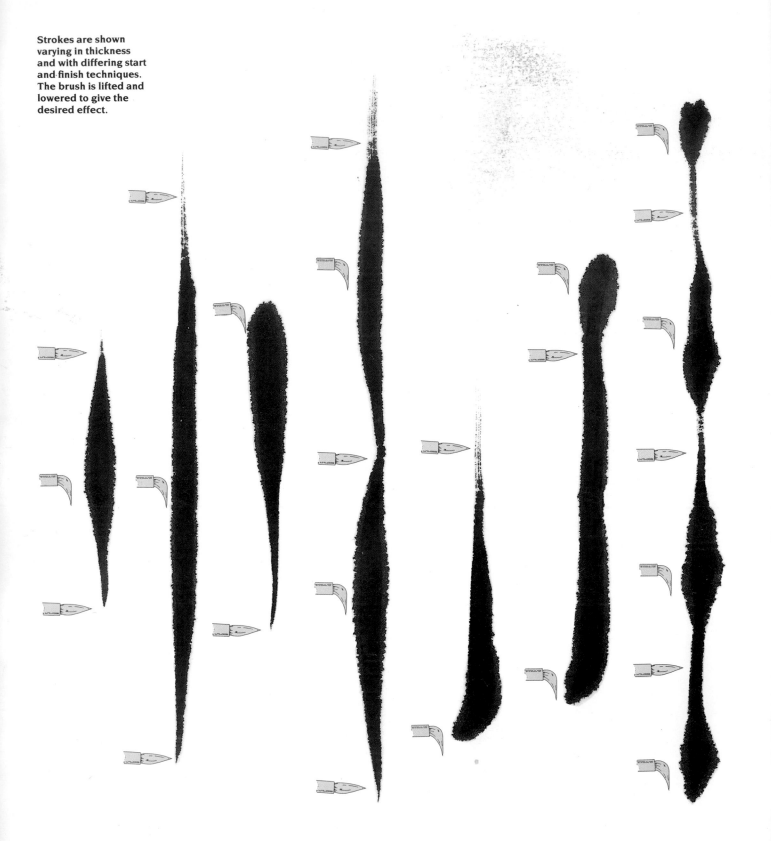

the side of the brush another. Similarly pushing it will be different from pulling it and simply leaving the brush on the paper for a few seconds whilst more ink is absorbed will give yet another effect. In all there are 18 different recognised lines – string, hair, wire, twisted, orchid leaf, tadpole etc, and also 30 types of dots – round, rock, rice, goose-pimple etc. Each painting can therefore be considered as an amalgam of these lines and dots, used with imagination and skill.

When you have practised producing strokes that are constant along their length, now try varying the thickness of the stroke. To achieve a point at the start, the brush must touch the paper as though coming out of the air. Gradually increase the pressure, moving all the time in one direction. Allow the brush to leave the paper back into the air again and you will have a point at both ends of the stroke, rather like a bamboo leaf. If the brush is lifted suddenly from the paper without resuming its vertical stance, a round-ended stroke will result. The way the brush is introduced to the paper and the way it leaves will affect the stroke. The pressure applied while the brush is in contact with the paper, and the speed with which the brush moves are all crucial to the end result. It may seem a lot to remember when you first start but it will soon become second nature.

BELOW LEFT A variety of short and long strokes can be used to create many subjects, especially flowers. By varying the way that the brush is pulled across the paper, several shapes can be made. Where long brushstrokes are required, variations in loading and pressure will create stunning effects. If more than one colour is used in the brush, these colours will gradually blend as more strokes are carried out with the one brush loading.

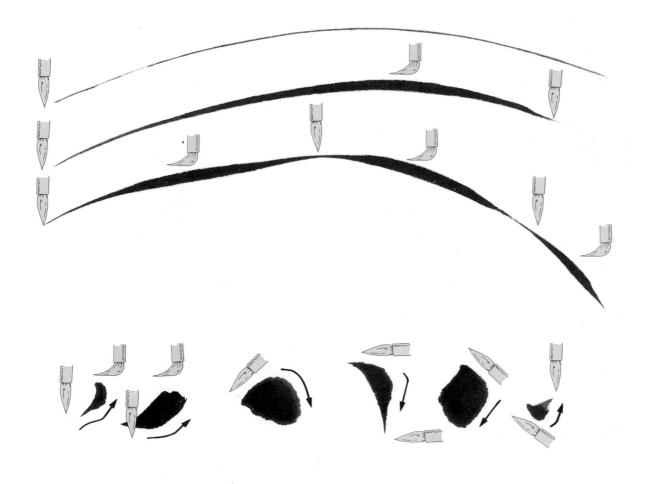

A SIMPLE PAINTING

Having practised various strokes, start putting them together to form flowers, rocks or animals. Try the simple cat in Chapter 8. You may think this is like a child's picture but it does involve wet strokes (not too wet) and markings going into previous strokes. A subject like this will test your powers of observation. Most beginners do not notice that the two sides of the cat are different, and produce an hourglass version! You may also find that the wet outline, where the water travels further than the ink, can cause problems when you add the whiskers. Copy the samples of flowers and leaves and try to put together a series of strokes into a recognizable shape. Remember that flowers turn in different directions and also face towards the sun. They will be at various stages of growth, and may even have petals missing.

LOADING THE BRUSH WITH COLOUR

Once you have practised with various shades of black, you can then move on to colours. When working with colours it is important to get the right balance between the levels of water and pigment.

Too much water and you will produce a stroke which is soft and pale, too much pigment and it will not all be absorbed by the paper.

Loading the brush with more than one colour will add interest to your painting. This involves placing different parts of the brush into various colours and should be used selectively.

Single brush loading is as it sounds – loading the brush with one colour or shade. For two colours, load an initial colour into the whole brush, wipe the tip firmly on the edge of the palette, and then load a second colour onto the 'clean' tip of the brush. Triple loading uses the brush in thirds – two colours in the main body of the brush and the third on the tip. Always wipe out the area of the brush destined for the next colour or it will not receive it sufficiently to register. It is better to use shades of one colour rather than different colours.

To paint structures such as bamboo stems, load the main body of the brush with yellow, then add black to two sides of the brush. This has the effect of creating a tube.

Practise these loadings and use them in the examples which follow. As you move around a flower structure, the colours will merge and blend, creating a more natural effect.

RIGHT **Single-brush loading – one colour in the brush. If the brush has previously been placed in water, and the colour is not blended fully into the brush, then a pale base will result. This effect can of course be used deliberately.**

FAR LEFT Tube loading
– the brush can be
loaded with the main
colour and then dipped
on two sides into a
darker colour. This will
create a tube-like
effect which will be
useful to describe
cylindrical shapes. This
method of loading will
need practice.

LEFT Double-brush
loading – first load the
brush with the main
colour, wipe the tip of
the brush against the
palette, and then load
the tip with the second
colour. This will give a
graded colour stroke if
shades of the same
colour have been used
as in this picture.

LEFT Triple-brush
loading – load the
brush with three
colours in equal thirds
of the brush. Judicious
use of this technique
with different shades
rather than contrasting
colours can add
interest and form to
your painting.

FLOWERS

OUTLINE

The outline technique for painting flowers is an ancient one. Once the whole painting – flowers, stems and leaves – were shown in outline. However solid stroke techniques began to be used for the leaves to contrast the robustness and strength of the leaves with the fragility of the flowers. Thus most flower pictures today use both techniques.

It is advisable to use a small brush when starting to paint using the outline technique. Once you are used to obtaining a fine light touch on the paper with the small brush a larger brush will give a better effect and the brush loading will last longer. Always start with the flowers themselves, separating the five petals (for plum) into groups of two and three.

RIGHT **Plum blossom is shown facing many directions. The strokes should be light and positive and carried out with a fine brush. The ink or paint could be either light or dark, but should in any case be dry rather than too wet.**

BELOW RIGHT **In painting a blossom branch, use a dry brush and hesitate at intervals to obtain a rough and gnarled appearance, changing direction slightly at each hesitation. If you are painting the branch before the blossoms, make sure you leave gaps in the branches where the flowers overlap.**

FAR RIGHT **The small delicate flowers of plum blossom make an ideal subject for outline painting – note the varied directions that the petals face. The outer line painted in stone green emphasizes the whiteness of the flowers.**

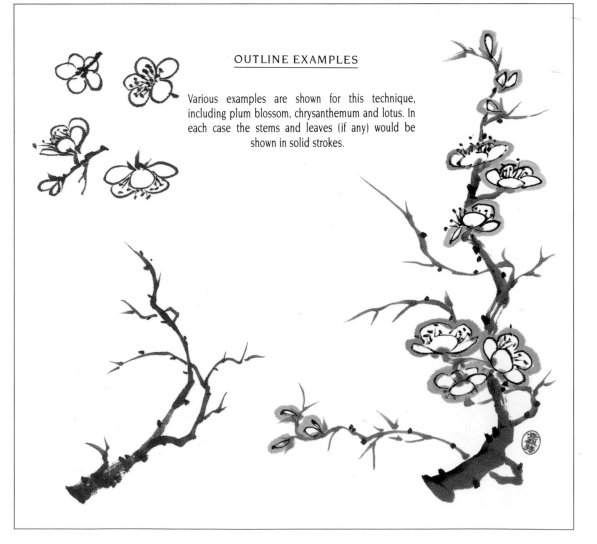

OUTLINE EXAMPLES

Various examples are shown for this technique, including plum blossom, chrysanthemum and lotus. In each case the stems and leaves (if any) would be shown in solid strokes.

Add the branches and stems next, with the brush travelling in the direction of growth, gradually lifting from the paper as you reach the outer, smaller twigs. Double loading can create an impression of the roundness of the branch; use the side of the brush with a darker colour to the tip. Some artists paint the branches first, leaving gaps for the blossom, but this is much more difficult if you are not used to visualizing the overall composition. The stems should be painted behind or in front of the flowers as blossom naturally grows from all sides of the branch.

As you paint the branch, use a dry, pushing stroke and hesitate at irregular intervals to enable the ink to spread further into the paper, thus creating nodes for the side branches or flowers. By altering the direction of the stroke slightly at each hesitation you will achieve a stem that is more in character with the subject. M*i* dots – first used by an artist called Mi Yuan Chang – can be added to the stem in very black ink. These help to increase the sense of roughness. Try to achieve a more natural, uneven distribution of dots.

Finally the stamens and any colour you wish to use can be added. The stamens are created by short flicking strokes working outwards from the centre. Try to visualize the direction the flower is facing and paint the stamens accordingly.

Colour can be added to the petals, as a line just inside or outside, the outline, or colour may be hinted at by partially shading the flower as with the Datura flowers.

FAR LEFT Chrysanthemum flowers can be painted in outline style. The petal is created in two strokes, from tip to centre. Fill in the colour with a single stroke. These flowers should be painted in differing scales and attitudes.

ABOVE LEFT For antler shaped branches and stems, start the stroke at base and push upwards with firm strokes. The use of curving lines as opposed to straight lines will create a different shrub or tree.

CENTRE LEFT AND BOTTOM In order to paint the outline of lotus flowers, first contour in grey, then tip in black over the top. If solid strokes are used, the petals can be painted in one or two strokes and lines added on the top as shown, painted down from the tip of the petal.

MAGNOLIA

To paint magnolia use a heavily sized paper and a meticulous technique. Because the ink will not run into the paper appreciably, the petals and stems are easy to paint – almost like drawing with a brush. Be careful to make the strokes interesting and not absolutely even in thickness. Paint the outline of the flowers and leaves first. If solid strokes are used, say in the branch, then these follow. After the ink has dried, colour can be added using a special technique. Load one brush with the darkest colour, another with either a lighter version of the same colour or clear water. As you add colour to either the tip or base of the petals, brush it out with the other brush. Tackle one petal or area at a time, making sure you get the appearance as even as possible. As the paper is well sized, the paint will stay on top for quite a while, therefore be careful not to smudge the shading with your hand. White or a paler colour can be worked in from the opposite edge of the petal when the first colour is dry. Again make sure it is spread evenly and the first colour can be darkened to add emphasis.

Silk which has been backed with paper is very similar to meticulous paper yet slightly more absorbent. Painting silk is often a beautiful ivory or cream colour, and sometimes old gold. If white is used as part of the magnolia petal it will show up beautifully against the faint colour.

With a more absorbent paper, outline strokes are more difficult and need a much lighter touch. Again make sure that they are not too even. With this paper there will be a greater contrast between the two techniques.

1 **ABOVE** The outline of the flowers is painted using an upright fine brush with the ink very much under control. Greater control is possible by using a small brush, which requires more frequent brush loading than a larger brush.

2 **ABOVE** Stems and branches are added in solid strokes. Interrupt the flow of the stroke to achieve a thickening or joint. The branches can be painted in either black or dark brown, or a mixture of the two colours. Small buds etc, can be added in yellow/green as required.

3 **ABOVE** Vary the colour shading by using a darker colour at the base and underside of the petals, or in the depths of the flower. As the paper is more sized and less absorbent, you should be able to spread the colour before it soaks into the paper.

WATERLILY FAN

Fan paper is available ready made but not fixed to the sticks. The texture of the paper and the fact that it has been made up dictates that it is of a meticulous type, so the techniques described for the magnolia can all be used.

Paint the outline first, gradually working across the surface. A fan composition is not easy to handle but if space is considered all the time, the results are very pleasing. Next colour the flowers, working on one petal at a time. The leaves follow and then any other detail such as the dragonfly. There is no need to show the surface of the water provided the plants appear to be growing naturally.

Once the painting is finished and dry, slide the fan sticks into the pockets between the two layers and glue the end covers into place. Make sure the fan opens and closes properly, and that the sticks are in the right pockets. Look at the example and you will see that the right-hand cover stick is fastened to the top of the fan, and the left-hand one to the underside.

1 LEFT Paint the outline onto the fan paper using an upright brush and minimal loading. Try to create interesting lines and strokes by varying the pressure.

2 RIGHT Add colour to the petals, starting with the tip and working the colour out halfway down the petal with a damp brush. The surface of the fan is much the same as the meticulous paper, and therefore the same techniques may be used.

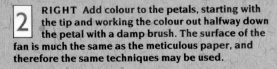

3 LEFT Complete the colouring of the leaves, again working the colour with two or more brushes. Use differing colours so that the leaves and flowers do not appear too bland.

RIGHT **A detail of the finished fan.**

BELOW **The completed fan mounted on sticks. The fan shape has been popular in China for centuries. Although many fans were used for ceremony and for cooling, they were also used as a painting format. You will often see fans in exhibitions which have never been mounted on sticks for traditional use, but are still in their flattened form, with or without the pleats or folding. The shape is a difficult one for painting within but very satisfying when complete.**

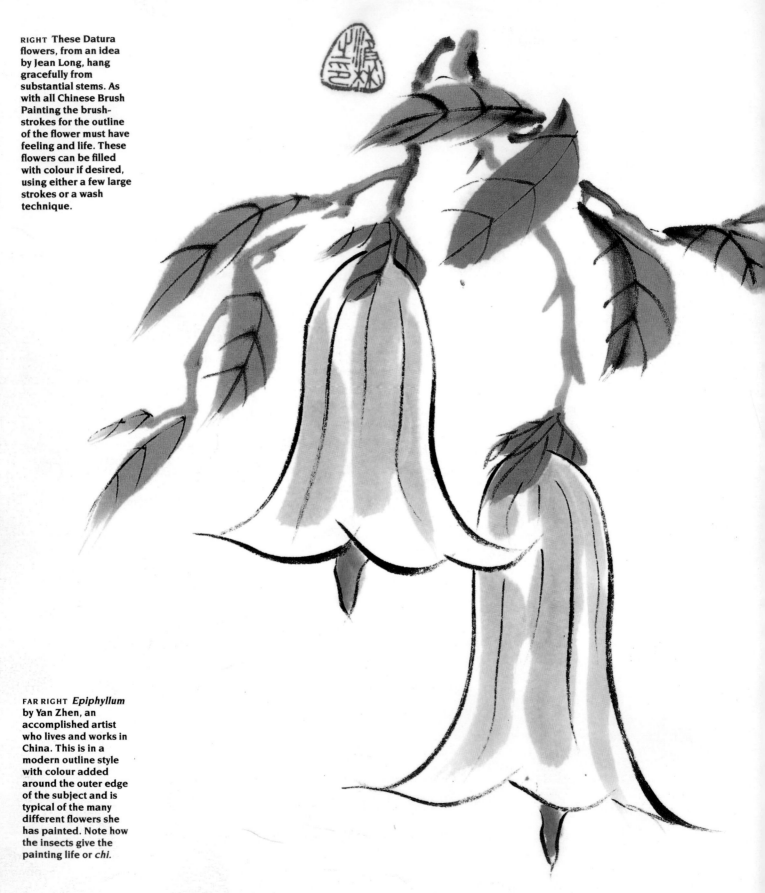

RIGHT **These Datura flowers, from an idea by Jean Long, hang gracefully from substantial stems. As with all Chinese Brush Painting the brush-strokes for the outline of the flower must have feeling and life. These flowers can be filled with colour if desired, using either a few large strokes or a wash technique.**

FAR RIGHT *Epiphyllum* **by Yan Zhen, an accomplished artist who lives and works in China. This is in a modern outline style with colour added around the outer edge of the subject and is typical of the many different flowers she has painted. Note how the insects give the painting life or** *chi*.

FLOWER SYMBOLISM

In Chinese paintings flowers have many symbolic meanings. Almond blossom and narcissus (good fortune), azalea, cherry and jasmine (ladies), blue hydrangea (colour of wisdom), camellia and plum blossom (good luck), camellia and wax blossom (hope and endurance), cherry blossom and magnolia (spring), convolvulus (love and marriage), chrysanthemum (autumn, retirement, pleasure, October, scholar, hermit and joviality), day lily (mother), early rose (winter), flag iris (summer), flowering plum (longevity, old age, hope, purity, winter, fortitude, January,

springtime and renewal), gardenia (November), jasmine and magnolia (sweetness), lotus (purity, summer, July, creativity and fidelity), magnolia (May), mallow (September), narcissus (good fortune), orchid (many children, piety, beauty and love), peach blossom (February), peony (good fortune, riches, rank, spring, affection and honour), pinks (summer), poppy (December), tree peony (spring, March), yellow hibiscus (triumph of summer).

These hidden meanings can be used to add an extra touch to paintings and gifts.

RIGHT **A lily painted on sized Xuan by the author. After painting the outline in fine strokes, add the colouring using the same technique as for the magnolia. The leaves are painted in solid strokes.**

FAR RIGHT **An outline magnolia on meticulous paper by David Hirst. David used a standard outline version by the author as a guide, but by using sized Xuan paper he achieved a different result.**

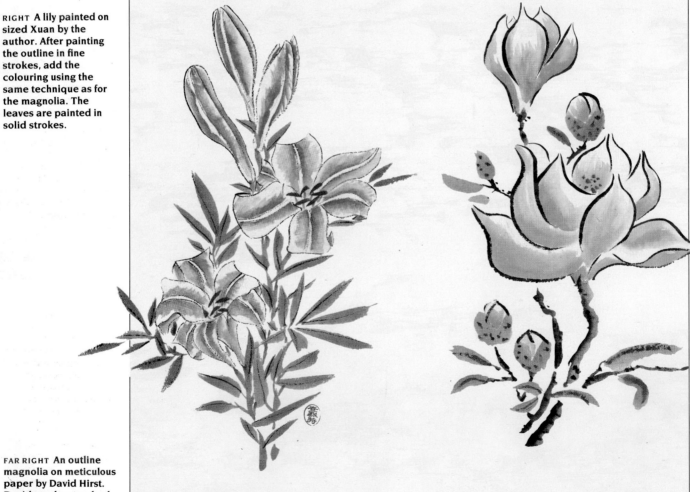

SOLID STROKE

When painting flowers, try to create a picture of the flower in your mind, from nature, from a photograph, or from a sketch. Ideally you should study a flower carefully noting the number of petals, their shape and the way they grow out from the stem. Examine the centre of the flower and decide what the most recognizable features are. Check what the veins on the leaves look like, how they branch outwards. When you know how the whole plant looks, then you are ready to paint.

To create a flower in Chinese style, each petal and leaf can be painted in a series of solid strokes. Each stroke should make a statement about the flower. By assembling these strokes in a variety of ways, the individual florets can be made to face in differing directions. In nature, the flowers turn upwards to face the sun, or hang down in graceful groups. In the examples you will see that the character of the flower is carefully used to make the painting lifelike.

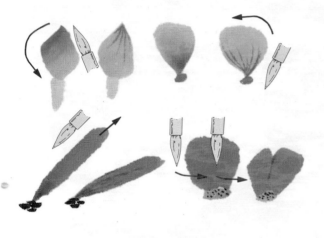

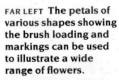

FAR LEFT The petals of various shapes showing the brush loading and markings can be used to illustrate a wide range of flowers.

LEFT Use small flick strokes starting from centre outwards to create the sunflower-shaped flower. The tip of the brush should hit the paper first and then flick off with a wrist-twisting action.

FAR LEFT To create a petal shape or flower the tip of the brush should be positioned at the centre of flower and loaded with a darker colour. Buds are the opposite way round with the darker colour and tip at the point.

LEFT In creating the lotus shape the tip of the brush is used to form the tip of the individual petals and the point of the bud. The brush should be pulled slightly sideways to get the wider petal shape.

RIGHT **Chrysanthemums require shorter more abrupt strokes than most flowers. Using a small brush, flick the brush towards the centre of the flower. The brush should be applied more firmly to the paper than when painting the sunflower petal shape.**

FAR RIGHT **A flick stroke is also used for painting poinsettias. However, a bigger brush is required to create wider petals.**

CENTRE RIGHT **In order to create the almost square shape of the rose leaf the brush is placed on the paper with the point upwards. The brush is then moved down and sideways at the same time.**

RIGHT **To create orchid-style leaves, apply the paint using the brush as if it were a pendulum. The brush should be lowered while travelling over the paper so that the initial contact with the paper is very light.**

FAR RIGHT **In order to make the leaves twist along their length, lift the brush slightly and then press down again to vary the width of the leaf.**

FAR LEFT This spray of leaves shows how little of the stem need be shown if the leaves are arranged naturally. The leaf stroke should travel sideways and lengthways at the same time, and the tip of the brush lifted off the paper at the end.

LEFT Gouache is used here to add white veins to the cyclamen and ivy leaves. The last leaf is carried out in three strokes – with the tip of the brush at the base of the leaf, the brush then travels 180 degrees in a circular motion to complete the three leaves.

LEFT When painting three-stroke leaves, start with the centre leaf then paint the two remaining leaves. With the tip of the brush at the base of the leaf work to the tip of the leaf then add the various arrangements of veins.

FAR LEFT This spray of leaves involves sliding the brush along the paper, away from the base, and gradually lifting the brush away from the paper in a curved motion. The differing pressure creates the varying shades.

LEFT A shorter leaf version with more veins. The veins on these shorter leaves are straighter than most and should start at the centre line and extend out to the edge of the leaf.

ORANGE CLIMBER

This plant climbs upwards and hangs gracefully out from its support with the flowers turning towards the sun. To paint the plant successfully, you need to express this elegant growth pattern.

After mixing, blending and loading the brush with shades of yellow and orange, or orange and red, use a wedge-shaped stroke to form the petals into flower shapes, each one different from the last.

Show the flowers in different stages of development from buds to full bloom.

Next add the leaves, again blending and mixing colours to give interest and character to your painting. Now paint the stems, making sure you are conscious of the spaces you are creating and that you retain the essence of the plant. Lastly add veins to the leaves and stamens to the flowers. The darker colour gives definition to the painting.

1 ABOVE LEFT Start by painting the flowers and buds. The tip of the brush should point to the top of the bud, and to the centre of the flower. Paint petals in groups of two and three, as this helps to enhance the natural look of the flowers.

2 ABOVE Add the leaves, remembering that some of the leaves should be placed in front of the stems. Careful positioning of these leaves can cover up much of the stem/branch and result in a natural-looking composition.

3 LEFT Add the stems, hesitating with the brush to create small nodules. Add two small strokes beneath the buds and flowers for the calyx.

4 **BELOW** Complete the painting by adding the veins on the leaves, stamens on the flowers and a seal. The main emphasis should be on a lively painting with the composition of the flowers correct for their growing style.

DICENTRA

This flower is also known as Dutchman's Trousers, or Bleeding Heart (because of its heart-shaped flower). It is not a traditional Chinese flower, however, the Chinese Brush Painting techniques, can be applied to any flower, animal or bird, whether traditional Chinese or not.

Mix together shades of red and pink, and form the brushstroke as shown. Group the strokes in pairs, positioning them to give an arching spray.

With a lightish green, add the leaves using three strokes for each one. The stems are in reddish brown, again accentuating the arching nature of the spray. Details such as veins, and centres are added last.

Any plant whose branches hang can look graceful and delicate. Avoid using too much pigment or you will destroy the transparency of the watercolours, and make it difficult to mount your painting traditionally.

1 LEFT The petals consist of two strokes. Curve the brush around the top and then down to give a point on each side. Vary the size of the flowers along the stem.

2 BELOW LEFT Add the three-stroke leaves in light green, making sure that they have sufficient substance and do not droop too much. Try also to vary the shades of green to add interest.

3 BELOW RIGHT The stems are painted in red/brown and consist of a series of curved strokes, keeping the brush in contact with the paper all the time. Work towards the tip of the flower stem.

4 **ABOVE** Complete the painting by adding veins on the leaves and the small stamen. The white stamens created by the outline technique look particularly effective.

BAMBOO

The examples here are all by the Chinese artist Qu Lei Lei, who paints and exhibits in England. Bamboo is said to be the hardest subject to paint and to the Westerner it is, along with the orchid, perhaps the most typically Chinese subject.

When painting bamboo, you must consider the way of growth, age and situation of the plant. Will you be showing the whole plant or only a section? Is it the bottom or top of the plant? This is important as the segments or distances between the nodes vary quite dramatically. Near the ground the stem has short lengths between nodes, increasing as you look up the plant and returning to short segments in the new growth at the top.

The side shoots supporting the leaves join the main stem on alternate sides. The stem above the node must be narrower than the section underneath. Techniques for painting stems vary from north to south in China. Some use fat strokes for the stems, others use thin strokes; sometimes the side of the brush is used or the brush is held upright. There are a few artists who use a 100mm hake brush to carry out a very large painting.

By careful brush loading, the cylindrical nature of the stem can be suggested, either by loading the tip of the brush with darker ink when using the brush sideways, or by adding the same to the sides of the brush if using a pushing stroke.

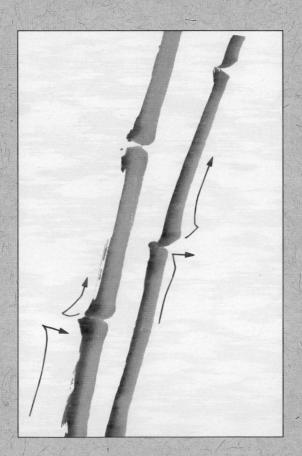

1 **ABOVE** Using an upright brush and starting from the bottom of the paper, push the brush upwards, moving to the left as a node is reached. When the brush is applied to the paper again, move it to the right and then upwards.

2 **ABOVE** Add the node markings in 'burnt ink' so that emphasis is given to the joints and they are made to appear stronger. There must be a marked contrast between the stem colour and that of the markings.

3 ABOVE Complete the painting with the addition of side branches and leaves. Good bamboo is very difficult to accurately reproduce and is not always painted in a static stance but may be windblown or covered in snow. It is often shown with a moon in the background or with other plant material. Sometimes rocks are incorporated into the composition.

LEFT **These examples of leaf groups have such names as 'landing goose' and 'flying swallow' which accurately describe their shape. It is essential that the leaves are painted with a life force and are not made to look like a bunch of bananas!**

The leaves and the general attitude of the plant will depend on the weather and the growing season. Is the bamboo in flower? Is it raining or snowing? Has the bamboo recently been buffeted by vicious winds – enough to tear the ends of the leaves, or is it in windy conditions and all flowing one way? Think about all these variations before and during your painting.

In the examples Qu Lei Lei has painted the stems first, then the leaves separately to show various groupings. Some of these have traditional names such as flying swallow and landing geese.

Make sure there is sufficient shading in the ink tones, and that the leaves have substance. If the plant is young, the leaves will point upwards and be quite stiff. As the plant ages they turn downwards but never look limp.

Chinese artists often have their own favourite subjects and in the past well known *literati* painters spent their whole lives just painting bamboo, often in a single colour. Some were famous for using red, green or purple to paint this plant although in general the most traditional way to paint bamboo is in shades of black ink. There is a legend that the first bamboo painted was inspired by the silhouette of the plant on a paper window covering cast by moonlight.

Western artists find it difficult to leave sufficient space in their work, especially with this subject. There is a temptation to keep adding more leaves. Look carefully at the completed painting and try to emulate the spaces and the general 'feel' of the plant. To achieve a good painting of bamboo is very satisfying.

**FAR LEFT Pansies in
solid stroke style. The
important feature to
note when painting
pansies is the position
of the top two petals –
one behind the other.
Other varieties (with
faces) can be painted
with a little
imagination.**

**LEFT Azaleas are
graceful flowers which
require soft brush
loading to recreate the
gentle, transparent
colours. All aspects of
the flowers should be
shown – buds, half-
open flowers as well as
full blooms to give
fullness to the
composition.**

The emphasis in painting flowers in the
Chinese style, using either outline or solid stroke
techniques, is on achieving a composition of flowers,
leaves and stems which is both graceful and elegant and above all natural.

FRUIT AND VEGETABLES

The Chinese enjoy painting all kinds of fruit, both arranged on plates and dishes or still hanging on the tree or plant. Some artists specialize in showing the bloom on grapes or a spot of light on the surface. Traditional patterns and shapes are used for the plate or dish. Careful brush loading is used to produce signs of ripening.

FRUIT

The techniques employed in painting fruit are similar and usually consist of one or two strokes with a carefully loaded brush. For single-stroke fruit the brush is placed on the paper with the tip of the brush to the centre of the fruit. The brush is moved in either a clockwise or anticlockwise direction, leaving the tip in the centre, until a solid circle has

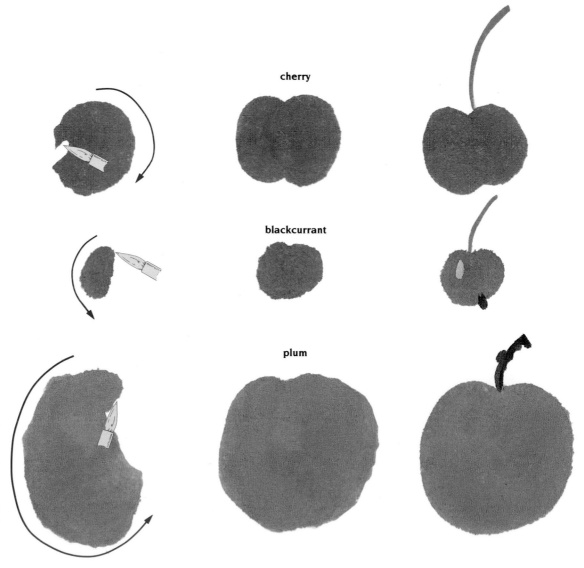

cherry

blackcurrant

plum

RIGHT AND OPPOSITE TOP All four of these fruits can be painted with two strokes. Either side may be painted first — experiment to find which is easiest. In choosing the colours try to remain faithful to the original colour of the fruit.

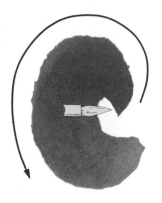

peach

Plums

been formed. Some artists have considerable skill and are able to leave a small area of white paper to one side to suggest a highlight on the fruit. When grouping fruit, ensure that some are closer together than others to achieve a natural arrangement. This is especially important with grapes and similarly shaped fruit.

When using the two-stroke technique, load the brush with a darker colour to the tip. The point of the brush can then be placed either to the outside or to the centre of the fruit – one method will give a darker outline and is more popular, the other will produce a darker centre.

Stems, details and leaves can be added as for flowers. The attitude of the leaves and stems is important to achieve the correct balance. In the examples, different sizes of fruit have been used from raspberries and blackcurrants to peaches.

LEFT AND BELOW Although most fruit will hang downwards because of its weight compared to the stem or branch, the composition will be more interesting and true to life if the fruit is painted from different angles.

cherry

peach

Rambutan

lychee

grapes

loquats

RIGHT, FAR RIGHT AND CENTRE Unlike the previous examples, these fruits are completed with one stroke. The tip of the brush is placed to the centre of the fruit and the heel taken around in a circle. With careful brush loading, natural variations in shade can be achieved.

RIGHT Fruit leaves should vary in length, width and perspective. As with the flower leaves, a natural pose and grouping will help the appearance of your painting and will also enable stems to be shown passing behind leaves.

LEFT **As is the case with other fruit, the stems of the lychees should look capable of supporting the bunches of fruit. A more interesting and natural composition will be achieved by placing the start of the branch off-centre along the sides of your piece of paper.**

RIGHT **Dots are used to create the individual raspberries. To enhance the realism of the picture vary the size and shape of the individual sprays. Try to ensure that the berries look full and juicy. The vivid contrast in colour and the size of the fruit make raspberries ideal for paintings or cards.**

FAR RIGHT **The stiffness of the branch provides a sharp contrast to the curves of the cherry stems. A typical depiction of cherries showing a careful arrangement of berries, both served on a plate and standing on the table, strongly echoes the style of classic still life compositions of Western art.**

RIGHT **Painting plums requires careful loading of the brush. Load the brush with the appropriate colour and then dip the tip of the brush into a darker paint. Let the tip of the brush travel around the outside of the fruit. Again the colouring is important and there are several varieties of plum to paint.**

LEFT By placing one cluster of peaches on top of the other the composition is given extra length and perhaps elegance. Because the fruit changes colour as it ripens, the choice of shades is wider allowing greater variation in the composition. Paint the fruit first, followed by the leaves and finally the stems. The left hand seal reads, 'enjoy a little leisure from a busy day'.

VEGETABLES

These are also favourite subjects for Chinese Brush Painting and are used as a sign of plenty. They vary from beans and other similar shapes hanging from the vines, to water chestnuts, mushrooms and chinese leaves. The latter appear in many paintings and are often carved on brush pots and other scholars' desk items.

When painting vegetables, try to vary the strokes and ink tones. Both solid and outline techniques should be used to add liveliness, and vary the use of wet and dry strokes. Carrots are painted in a single stroke – starting with the wide end and a sideways brush, gradually moving onto the tip of the brush at the root end.

It is best to treat your copying as a detective exercise, looking for changes in stroke, tone and repetition to find out how the shape was built up and where the strokes start and end. In time you will be able to look at a shape and know instinctively how to form it. You can then include far more of your feelings about the subject in the painting.

RIGHT **Favourite subjects are often the most ordinary objects. Vegetables, especially Chinese leaves or cabbage, allow the full use of both outline and solid strokes. This painting is on Yuan shu paper which has a rich yellow colour. The contrast of the thin and thick strokes has a special impact on this paper.**

ABOVE, CENTRE AND
BELOW It seems ironic
that the most mundane
vegetables may be the
subject of one of the
most elegant art forms.
However, even simple
vegetables can provide
inspiration! Use the
brushstrokes to show
the bulges or structure
of the fruit. Subjects
such as garlic and
shallots are often tied
together at the top.

SYMBOLISM OF FRUIT AND VEGETABLES

Fruit plays a major part in New Year and other special celebrations. Common meanings are – apples (peace), apricots and cherries (fair lady, April), Buddha's-hand citron and oranges (good fortune and immortality), peaches (longevity, spring and marriage), pears (August), persimmons (joy), plums (hope, January, good fortune, purity and longevity), pomegranates (fertility, many sons, June, posterity).

Vegetables – fungus (longevity, fertility, immortality), gourds, (longevity).

BIRDS AND
INSECTS

Birds and insects are used extensively as subjects for Chinese Brush Painting. They are used to introduce exotic interest and sometimes humour and are usually shown with flowers, trees, fruit and other animals. Birds often have symbolic meaning and more than one theme can be included.

When painting birds it is important that they appear to sit firmly on a branch or rock, be steady in flight and, if several are shown, be in different attitudes to give liveliness to the painting.

Birds are often chosen for their humorous or predatory qualities: they might be cheeky sparrows, or a large, fierce eagle. The expression in the eye is often used to give the main impact. The artist Fu Hua often uses the eye and the overall attitude of the bird to affect the viewer in various ways. The golden pheasant by Fu Hua certainly causes a reaction in most people who view it, whether artists or not. Some of his paintings are very large and one has to stand a long way back to appreciate them.

RIGHT **Humour is an essential part of many Chinese Brush paintings, as these cheeky sparrows show.**

This delightful
pheasant by Fu Hua is
full of humour and life.
Fu Hua regularly
paints, demonstrates
and exhibits in
England. The colour of
the rock is unusual and
evokes much comment.
The simplicity of some
of the strokes is offset
by the detail in the tail
feathers.

DUCKS

Ducks, especially Mandarin, are symbols of marriage and often painted as a pair or a group. Mandarin ducks are sometimes painted with solid strokes, but the three illustrated are in outline style. Their whiteness can be accentuated by including some background scenery.

Ducks in water are sleek and assured, moving with ease. Ducks on land are awkward and comical, their webbed feet striving for balance. White ducks are mainly domesticated, seen either lazily swimming around or loaded into cycle panniers, baskets and onto the tops of buses on their way to market.

Shape and movement are all important for these ducks. Start with the eye, then the back line of the beak. Next put in the rest of the beak followed by the head and neck. Work from neck to wings, then tail. The underparts and feet are put in last with the colour on beak and feet.

RIGHT **Differing arrangements of birds can give amusing scenes as these ducks show. Often it is the position of the head or the eye which can almost provide its own caption! A variety of poses of these birds would make a wonderful frieze for a child's room. Start with the eye, then the back line of the beak. Next paint the rest of the beak followed by the head and neck. Continue from the neck to the wings, then the tail. The underbelly, and feet are painted last. Finish by colouring the beak and feet.**

SPARROWS

These are small, cheeky birds, always giving a sense of mischief and squabbling. Those shown in the example are a simple version which is easy to master. Just by changing the direction of the beak and eyes you can completely change the character or mood of the bird.

First paint a horizontal stroke for the head. Then add two vertical strokes with width in the centre (by applying more pressure to the brush), ending with a point at the wing tips. Starting at the bottom of the tail, flick the brush up in two long strokes to form the tail feathers. All these strokes can be in black, grey or brown ink as you wish. With a fine brush and dry black ink add the beak, eyes and feet. A few dots can be added to the breast area followed by, a light coloured stroke with a side-ways brush over the top. Complete the picture by adding a branch or grass stem for the bird to sit on.

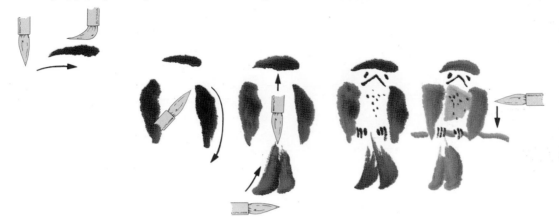

LEFT **Freestyle sparrows can be painted in five stages as shown here. Use a brush large enough to add some substance to the wings, then change to a smaller one for the eyes, beak, spots and claws (painted in that order). Return to the larger brush for the breast and branch.**

LEFT **Groups or pairs of birds provide interesting subject matter for larger compositions. The expressions and characters can be altered subtly by varying the shape of the eye and beak.**

RIGHT The detail of an expressive bird on a willow branch is from a scroll by Gang Mei. The rest of the painting is purely suggestive but the viewer's eye takes in the probable position of the river bank and the direction of the current.

ABOVE **A painting of a kingfisher and reeds on mulberry paper by the author. The success of the thick mulberrry paper lies in the opportunity it offers to use dry strokes thus allowing greater control and definition of the shape of the bird.**

RIGHT **This ibis, in the style of Han Meilin, is almost cartoon in character. Meilin's compositions are often comic rather than serene. The pale strokes are painted first followed by the darker strokes.**

BIRDS BY OTHER CHINESE ARTISTS

There are many ornate small and large birds shown in easily available books, especially from Hong Kong. Whilst some artists produce technically accomplished and accurate bird paintings, other artists choose to let the character of the bird distinguish the picture.

Fu Hua fills a painting or scroll with his birds, often to a large scale. The pheasant and crane are two such paintings.

Dai Ying paints a variety of subjects, but the most endearing are his water birds. Some examples are shown here and also in Chapter 14, where the technique is described. Although the method is an easy one his control is expert. By allowing the ink to run so far and no further, he creates many intriguing effects.

Han Meilin paints many animals as well as birds and is well known for his distinctive style.

LEFT **This small bird on a lotus leaf stalk is by Dai Ying, who lives in China but has also exhibited elsewhere. The posture of the bird is full of life and joy.**

RIGHT A pair of small birds painted by Han Meilin for Qu Lei Lei. Pairs of birds often symbolize peace, harmony and a happy marriage, reflecting a popular Western theme.

若人春靈取來住
有知去喚歸同
已年月林
禾六美作

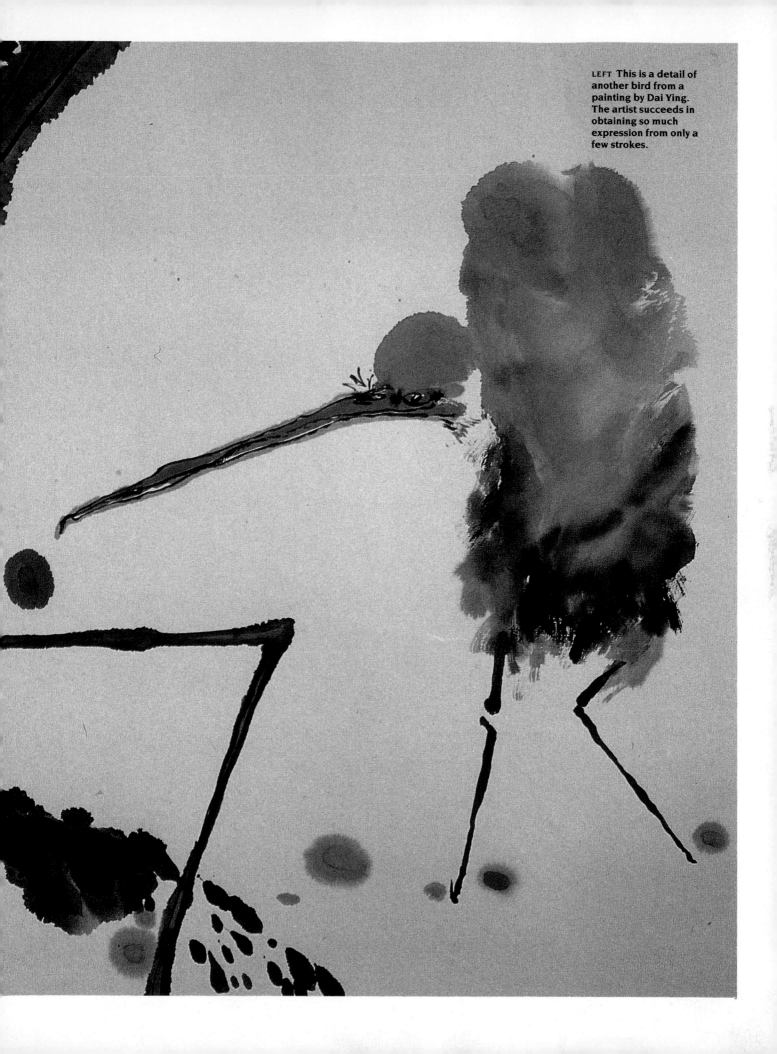

INSECTS

FAR RIGHT AND BELOW
Insects provide particularly intricate and complex subject matter and thus offer an interesting and lively contrast in pictures composed primarily of few of simple brushstrokes. In complex pictures the effect may be of overcrowding.

These are included in many paintings, sometimes with flowers, or fruit. They often introduce an extra dimension into the painting and can also disguise the odd spot of ink on the paper! Insects can be painted in meticulous or free style. When choosing a suitable insect to include, be sure to keep it in scale with the rest of the painting.

The choice of technique is rather personal, but try to introduce some variety. A lively and interesting painting should be your aim – this need not depend only on the subject matter, but can come from the methods used.

FAR RIGHT CENTRE
Butterflies look particularly attractive when painted in outline style as these examples show.

BELOW **The praying mantis looks almost comic with its huge eyes.**

LEFT This detail from a painting by Yan Zhen shows how she has incorporated the insects into the picture. The minimal amount of detail shown for the insects complements the painting style generally.

RIGHT **This spiders web by the author – inspired from more than one source – shows how flowers and insects can be interlinked. In this composition the web serves to draw attention to the spider whilst the foliage frames the picture.**

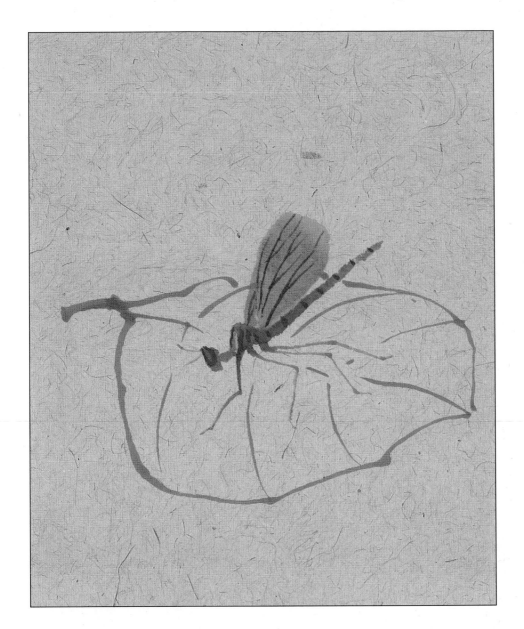

LEFT **The wing of this dragonfly is formed from a single stroke and the markings added when totally dry. The legs should be painted with a fine, upright brush and the leaf painted last of all.**

SYMBOLISM OF BIRDS AND INSECTS

Birds used as symbols include cock (courage, virtue, life force, the sun and warmth), crane (youth, longevity good fortune and promotion), crow (ill omen, filial piety), eagle (heroism), goose or ducks (marriage), kingfisher, pheasant and peacock (beauty), magpie (good omens), parrot (fidelity), quail (courage), phoenix (peace and prosperity), stork (longevity), swallow (future success). A pair of birds means peace, harmony and a happy marriage. A pair of peacocks symbolizes business prosperity.

Insects are also indicative of many values – bees (industry and hard work), butterflies (summer, autumn, conjugal felicity, joy, good luck, feminine, grace and light), cicada (eternal youth and happiness), cricket (summer and courage). A pair of butterflies shows nuptual harmony.

ANIMALS

When painting animals the character of the subject should be of paramount importance. An elephant must look very heavy and strong; a mouse small and light. The colour should be natural and the setting such that the animal looks right in it. There are many varieties of animal that can be painted, and not surprisingly some of those most often featured are the animals of the Chinese zodiac – rat, ox, tiger, rabbit or hare, dragon, snake, horse, sheep or goat, monkey, rooster, dog, and pig. When the Chinese New Year occurs, pictures of the various animals are available in the shops.

There are several ways of representing an animal, whether mythical or real; a careful meticulous painting, a free-style version, or a painting which is more like a cartoon or caricature. With all these different styles of painting it is essential to look at the animal and note particularly strong limbs, the shape and position of joints and other features such as ears, legs, paws, etc.

The surface texture is important too. An elephant requires smooth strokes to show its leathery hide, whereas a fluffy kitten needs much wetter strokes and more absorbent paper.

RIGHT **This unusual elephant painting, by Jennifer Scott gives the impression of strength and power with the muscles of the animal implied by the size and shape of the brushstrokes. The habitat is hinted at with a few strokes.**

DRAGON

This mythical creature appears in many cultures and varies mainly in the body shape, whether it is winged or not, and the number of claws.

In China the dragon has been used as decoration for centuries, and its correct appearance was a matter of life or death. Anyone apart from the Emperor showing a five clawed dragon on any of their possessions was executed. Other high ranking court officials were allowed four claws, while the rest of the court were allowed only three. The dragon is fifth in the cycle of twelve animals in the Chinese zodiac and is referred to as one of the four divine animals, with the phoenix, tortoise and unicorn. The dragon is said to be the bearer of the thunderbolts and to bring the celestial rain. A pair of dragons confront adversity and overcome it, a single dragon indicates goodness and strength,

and will bring good fortune to the home. A dragon is also associated with greed.

The dragon shares many features with other animals, among them python's body, fish scales and eagle's talons. The colour of dragons varies; those depicted on robes were often golden. Chinese dragons are majestic and sinuous – the body should flow across the painting.

Dragons are frequently shown chasing the pearl of wisdom and the illustrated example is no exception. First paint the head in fine lines, followed by the body and tail. Additional details and colouring are painted last. The main colour should be applied in the largest strokes possible; use a brush that is too large rather than one that is too small. Never 'scrub' the colour onto the paper – always use definite strokes, and as few as possible.

RIGHT **Using a fine brush, paint the main outline, starting with the head. Complete the outline, working towards the tail. With a mythological subject such as this you can exaggerate some of the features to great effect.**

BELOW **Colour in the dragon with as few strokes as possible, using yellow, green or red. Add some scales with a fine brush and show the dragon chasing the pearl of wisdom.**

PANDA

This is a simple version, not attempting to show too much detail but rather the shape and posture. The shape of the eye and ear strokes should be imitated as far as possible as these are two of the most recognizable features. The front limbs are not separate from each other in colour as the black area continues across the animal's shoulders and onto the other limb. Once the method of painting pandas has been mastered, illustrations and photographs can be used to compose a group such as that shown on the panda fan.

1 **ABOVE** There are five stages to painting a panda. Start with the eye(s), ears and nose in black ink. If painting a group then show them in differing attitudes and angles.

2 **ABOVE** Using the point of the large brush, or a finer one, with a little ink paint the outline of the face. Take care not to make the jaw line too distinct.

3/4 **ABOVE** With thick black ink add the front and rear legs, allowing the ink to spread for a fluffy outline. Claws can be added and the black markings extended across the shoulders so that the front limbs are linked. Some illustrations and models are inaccurate and do not show this.

5 ABOVE Finally add the fine lines for the back and belly, remembering to shade the lower abdomen. To make the picture more interesting provide some bamboo for the panda to eat, or maybe a rock for leaning against.

LEFT This detail of a panda face shows the amount of expression that can be incorporated into the eyes. The shape of the eye patch is quite distinctive.

FAR LEFT Fan paper is not very absorbent, therefore the large limbs of the animals are not so easy to paint. To overcome this a sideways brush has to be used to maximum advantage. As with flower compositions, groups of animals are only really successful when the positions and expressions are varied.

RIGHT This antelope painting by the author relies heavily on the style of Han Meilin. This style uses a variety of ink tones together with suggestive lines to gain the effect of life and movement.

ANTELOPE

This painting, in the style of Han Meilin, shows movement and structure. The light grey lines are painted first, followed by the darker detailing. It is important for the strokes to be carried out with confidence, especially the horns.

BOTTOM RIGHT The ears of the cat are painted first with the tip of the brush to the top and a sideways pull on the brush. The head consists of one horizontal stroke and three vertical. The body is carried out in two strokes, using an oblique stroke and starting at the neck. The second stroke starts below the first at shoulder level, and the brush is swirled around at the hip line. The tail is added next. While the ink is still wet, the stripes are painted in darker ink, together with the whiskers.

CAT

The two main features of a cat painting are the soft coat and the fluidity of movement. The painting by Jennifer Scott (opposite page) shows the stretching nature of a cat's stance. The strokes are almost calligraphic, and placed with care. The rear view of the cat has wet strokes with lines overpainted to suggest stripes. The softness is accentuated by the way the ink has been absorbed into the paper.

ANIMAL SYMBOLISM

The animal kingdom shows a wide range of meanings. Some of the most common are: bat (felicity and happiness), bear (bravery and strength), elephant, leopard and lion (energy and strength), dog (fidelity), fox, hare and deer (longevity), monkey (health and success), ox (springtime), rat (prosperity), sheep and goat (retired life), tiger (courage and energy), tortoise (longevity and strength).

LEFT A very elegant and expressive cat by Jennifer Scott, who specializes in animal and figure paintings. Her distinctive style suggests both smoothness of movement and softness.

FISH

ish are rarely shown with all their surroundings in detail. Provided the fish appears to be swimming, then the water will be taken for granted by the viewer.

Some fish move in a sluggish, lazy fashion, others hover and dart and it is these qualities that should be expressed. As with the flower and fish examples, some of the examples are not typically Chinese in origin.

RIGHT To paint these Siamese fighting fish, start with the mouth, eye and gill lines. With a sideways brush add colour to the head and put in the side fin. Paint the body in two strokes, one below the other, narrowing the tail. Again with a sideways brush, add the main fins and tail – in one stroke if possible, but no more than two.

LEFT **Paint the two front fins at an angle to the body. Add scales as dots or lines, or a mixture of both. Show any water weed that you wish. Finally illustrate the texture of the fins with a fine brush. The seal reads 'fishes' happiness'.**

SIAMESE FIGHTER

Anyone keeping tropical fish will know this variety. The males are more flamboyant and aggressive, especially towards each other and whilst more than one female may be included in a tank, there should be only one male. When in fighting mood, both sexes expand their gills to give a lion-like appearance. They tend to move a short distance and then stop, extending their fins for balance. Colouring is exotic, usually blues and reds. The examples show the male – the female has much smaller fins.

Start the picture by marking the eye and mouth in outline, then paint the fin nearest the gill in a single wedge stroke, with the tip of the brush towards the gills. Add the body in three strokes, then the top fin, tail and bottom fin. The two very expressive front under-fins are painted at varying angles. Lastly add texture to the fins and body. In the wild, these fish live in muddy waters, in the examples they are shown in slightly cleaner setting with water plants suggesting current and movement. In the second example, the fish is going up to the surface for air.

CARP AND SIMPLE FISH

Although some methods of painting fish are complex and skilled, the more simple versions are no less effective if they have some spontaneity. Start with the mouth and eye, followed by the back and belly strokes, then the fins and tail. Any details are added last.

The completed composition can include water plants and a varying number of fish. A variety of fish can be shown in one picture if you wish, but always consider the spaces that are left. Are they interesting in shape or too regular? Are your fish spaced equally? Were the water plants positioned simply to take up the remaining space?

3 ABOVE The back of the fish can be painted in two ways – either as a single stroke with one gradual variation of pressure or as three sideways strokes using the side of a drier brush and pulling down.

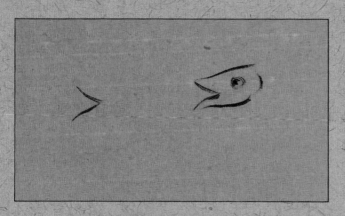

1 ABOVE Start with the mouth, eye and gills using a fine brush and dry ink. The lines should be smooth and flowing. Small gaps between the lines enhance the shape of the fish head.

4 ABOVE Complete the fish by adding spots on the back (before the paint is dry) and the lines on the fins (these are left until the paint is a little drier). It is these markings which help to add spirit and realism to the subject.

2 ABOVE Add the back and belly, followed by the tail and fins. Use extra pressure in the centre of the back stroke and gradually lift the brush up onto the tip again at the tail end. An oblique brush is swept from the body outwards, with the side of the brush in contact with the back for the fins, and the tip of the brush touching the body for the tail strokes.

5 ABOVE This picture shows a slightly different fish with a longer dorsal fin and two side strokes to the head. Many variations on this theme can be achieved and techniques for painting fish can be varied within a single composition.

LEFT The yellow colour of the grass paper complements the blue/ green shades of the painting. The expression of fishes is confirmed by the seal, which says 'Fishes' Happiness'.

83

CRABS

These crustaceans are a good practice subject for repetitious strokes! The examples clearly show how the crab is gradually built up, starting from the centre of the back. By creating the back in three strokes, the markings on the shell are formed rather than added later. The attitude of the legs and pincers can be very expressive. You should be aware of the spaces between the crabs and not make them too even.

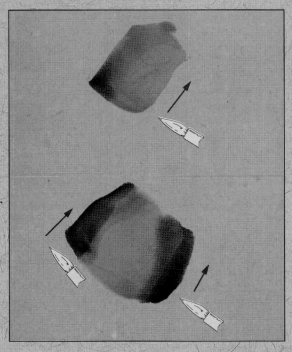

1 ABOVE Using an oblique brush, paint the centre of the back. Then add the side strokes, starting with an oblique brush and gradually lifting it to obtain the triangular shape.

3 ABOVE Add the legs, followed by the pincers. The angle between the upper leg and lower leg and between the upper leg and the body should be varied. It is this contrast that increases the excitement in the painting.

2 ABOVE With an upright brush flick into the body to form the eyes. To paint the claws lower the brush onto the paper gradually and lift it off sideways.

4 **ABOVE** Add more crabs to complete the composition, taking care all the while not to overcrowd the picture. This provides good practice at painting legs from all angles!

CATFISH

These fish are the clowns of aquarium, pond or river. Capable of great speed if they wish, they often hover and tumble in pairs. Although not brightly coloured, they have spots or stripes to help them merge into the background. They are non-aggressive and friendly. Being silt feeders they stay mainly at the bottom of their habitat, occasionally making fast spurts up to the surface.

The first example shows a talking catfish, so-called for the noises that it makes. This is a flat variety with very stiff, spiny fins. Use a sideways brush to make one stroke back from the position of the mouth, then add a stroke each side to give a blunt, diamond shape. Using the brush sideways, join the next stroke to the head, lifting the brush onto the tip as you approach the tail. Remember to curve the stroke as the brush travels over the paper. Paint in the fins, making sure that the junction with the body is kept narrow, and fanning outwards. While the wet is wet, add any spots and stripes so they blend with the body colour and do not stand out too much. As the body area is drying, put in the eyes and mouth details. This stage can be done first as in the Siamese fighter, but it is sometimes easier to get a good catfish expression if the eyes and mouth are left until later. Lastly add fine lines to show the ridges on the fins and whiskers. Water weeds can be included in the painting if you wish.

The second example shows a different variety, with a more vertical body and less width. It is painted in a similar order. Two strokes for the body (one top and one bottom), then the fins. Body markings follow, then eyes, ridges and whiskers. Again the water plants give the impression of current and movement.

GOLDFISH

This painting is in the Lingnan style and has had a coloured wash applied to the reverse. The fish were painted in a similar way to the previous examples (the body in two strokes and the tail in three strokes). The tails are made to appear more lacy and fragile by extending the veins beyond the tail strokes with dotted lines and adding white lines over the basic strokes with gouache. Careful and imaginative brush loading gives the darker line on the back and parts of the tail.

Once the painting is dry, you can apply a wash to the back. With fish as the subject you can also apply a wash to the front to increase the impression of water. First dampen the painting all over with a brush or spray – avoid soaking the paper by spreading the water well with a *hake* brush. Then apply the light colour. It is easy to add more coats, but you cannot take away a wash that is too dark! The example has a blue wash at the top of the painting, gradually changing to green at the bottom. The lower chop says 'fishes' happiness' – referring to a story from 1000 BC, when Zhuang Zi expressed his feelings about fish swimming in clean water. The chop, carved by Qu Lei Lei, uses bronze-age characters (2000 – 1000 BC).

FAR LEFT This pair of goldfish has been painted in Lingnan style, a style practised widely in southern China, Hong Kong and Singapore. Washes of blue and green have been added to the front of the painting, to increase the underwater effect. If this wash treatment had been applied to the back of the painting (as with a flower painting) then the water effect would have been less.

LEFT To achieve the wrinkled effect of the background the paper is crumpled and then roughly smoothed out again. A large, wet brush is drawn across the paper allowing the colour to soak into the high points but not the valleys between.

FISH SYMBOLISM

All types of fish have fascinating meanings. Any of them can mean conjugal felicity, happiness, harmony, revival, abundance, and wealth, while carp can indicate longevity and help dispel evil spirits. A pair of fish stand for a happy marriage; such a painting would make an unusual wedding gift.

FIGURE PAINTING

Figures can be the main subject of a painting or add atmosphere to a landscape. Differing sizes of figure involve different techniques.

Many figure paintings seen in the West on porcelain plates and in books are carried out by the meticulous method. This means that they are a more realistic, detailed interpretation and therefore more closely resemble Western art. They are often painstakingly coloured, with great detail in the folds of clothes and the features.

On the other hand free-style technique adds liveliness to a painting where the stance and attitude of the figure is the most important feature. Often, especially in small scale work, the face and limbs are just hinted at, and the rough shape of the clothes shown. It is the movement that counts.

A favourite subject in landscapes used to be *literati* gentlemen, shown in natural surroundings, either discussing poetry or generally enjoying the closeness of nature. Smaller figures were also depicted, which at first glance appeared to be children, but were in fact servants. Their lower station in life was illustrated primarily by their diminished size and clothing perhaps second.

The other factor which significantly influenced the scale of the figure was the Chinese belief in the importance of Heaven, and the insignificance of man. This belief also accounts for the excess of mounting material above a painting framed or mounted in oriental style. It is said that the most beautiful painting is a sheet of white paper, where you can change the image each day in your mind, or indeed escape from this world in contemplation.

There are many traditional subjects for figure painting. The ancient heroes such as Chung Kui, Li Kui and the gods such as Lao Shouxing (God of Longevity), often feature in Chinese Brush Painting. Scenes from classics such as *Dream of Red Mansions*

RIGHT *Chung K'uei,* **painted here by Jennifer Scott, is a figure from Chinese legend often illustrated in paintings. The costume is traditional and he is always shown with the same hat and tails.**

have provided the starting point for many paintings. However, the artist may find his freedom of imagination limited by the detail of the story and fixed preconceptions held by the viewer.

A better source of inspiration is everyday life in China, which covers such a wide variety of scenery, weather conditions, occupations and traditions. You will need to study closely books, calendars, and magazines – there has been a wealth of material published over the last few years, promoted by such a high interest in the East and its culture.

SMALL FIGURES

When painting a landscape with figures you will need to decide which to paint first – the setting or the figures. You may find it easier to put in the figures and the foreground first. Do not make the clothes too detailed, but make sure the pose is right. Are your figures looking up at a bird in flight, or at the moon? Are you painting a man standing on a raft with his cormorant, or a farmer following his water-buffalo in a flooded rice field? If you are painting the figure with solid strokes, do not make them too heavy. If using outline, keep the strokes rather dry and do not make the lines too even, leaving a gap here and there. Your figure should be standing securely either on raft or ground and should have the proper stance for rowing or walking. Gradually add more detail to the rest of the landscape, but try not to overcrowd it.

LEFT **This selection of figures shows the traditional way man is portrayed in Chinese Brush Painting. The figures are generally used in landscape work and need to have suitable action or stance to enhance or justify their incorporation into the scene. The colours should always be muted and should never dominate the landscape itself, thus reflecting the belief that man is insignificant when compared with nature.**

LARGE FIGURES

A large figure which dominates the painting requires a different approach. Unless the figure is turned away from the viewer, the face should be shown in greater detail. One method of starting is to load a brush with a flesh colour and paint a 'T' to indicate the forehead and nose. The eyes, nostrils and mouth can then be positioned. In a free-style painting of a figure, the clothes are suggested rather than shown in detail. Dark trousers or gowns can be illustrated with solid strokes as in the monk painting. The dry brushstrokes help to enliven the work and give the feeling of movement. If painting hands proves to be a problem, your figures could have their hands hidden by long sleeves. Feet are often concealed by a robe.

There are many examples of figures painted in the meticulous style which seem almost photographic in quality. These take a long time and great skill to execute.

RIGHT **A variety of strokes and ink tones are necessary for** *chi* **in a figure painting. The painting of a monk hurrying along, by the author, is enhanced by the contrast between the dry brushstrokes and the wetness of other strokes in the robes.**

FAR RIGHT **This** *Dancing Girl* **by Dong Chensheng (for Qu Lei Lei) is typical of his style; his figures are always so full of movement. This artist is particularly famous for his paintings of opera figures.**

RIGHT This figure, inspired by Fan Zeng, is obviously intrigued by the freshness of spring blossom. Note the lines of the clothes and the irregularity of the strokes. Fan Zeng's style has been simplified quite dramatically here.

The brushstrokes on
the robes need to be
simple and fluid: the
flow of the cloth
complements the
calmness of the figure
and thus increases the
somnolent air of the
painting. The softness
of the clothes
compared with the
ruggedness of rocks
also provides an
interesting contrast.

LANDSCAPE

BELOW **This exquisite album leaf, mounted as a scroll, is from the Ming Dynasty (1368 – 1644) and was shown at the Sydney L Moss Gallery exhibition in 1990. The brushstrokes in this painting are of superb quality and the traditional style of painting trees is excellent.**

In accord with the minimalist and symbolic nature of Chinese Brush Painting, Chinese landscapes are represented by just two characters – mountain and water. These really do describe the essence of most Chinese scenery: the majesty and rugged strength of the mountains contrasts with the fluid nature of waterfalls and lakes. Misty scenes are expressive of large areas of China and often feature in the different perspective views that are so special to Chinese scholars.

FAR LEFT This beautiful landscape scroll was painted by in 1942 by Pu Chuan, a member of the Qing Dynasty royal family, born in 1913 and thought to be living in USA. One of the seals on the bottom right-hand side means 'On my way to a friend, you can see ten miles of clouds and hear the rustle of the pine'. This is very descriptive of the feeling evoked by splendid landscapes.

LEFT This very restful landscape was painted, after very little tuition, by Brigid Nunan, a physically disabled student.

RIGHT As this painting shows a simple landscape can be formed from dots alone. Although the use of only dots may seem restrictive, variety can be incorporated into the painting by using all or a selection of the eighteen different dots which are recognized.

FAR RIGHT The use of lines creates a more realistic and, in this painting, a more dramatic effect. Again there are thirty different lines so that many interesting combinations can be used.

FAR RIGHT 'Pointed' mountains such as these give a feeling of drama and danger.

CENTRE Whereas 'blunt' mountains give a more benevolent feeling of softness.

ABOVE This style of rock illustration is an imitation of the veins that are often used on lotus leaves, and is carried out with a small upright brush. It is the variation of styles and strokes which helps to build up an interesting landscape.

To understand some of the unusual aspects of the traditonal landscape it is essential to appreciate the importance of Heaven and Nature compared with the relative unimportance of man.

Rocks and trees are textured and detailed to suggest their structure and form. Many of these techniques have been adapted and used in Western graphic art. Landscapes are built up in a more layered way than flower paintings for example (unless using a meticulous style).

In the first examples, the landscapes contain either dots or lines. However, most landscapes consist of various combinations of these two.

Chinese landscapes are painted with different perspectives to those common in the West. They are known as high, deep or level perspective. A high viewpoint accentuates the grandeur of nature and this is apparent in many traditional paintings in books and museums.

The elegant painting by Pu Chuan shows the effect of misty space. The ink tones and brush strokes subtly suggest the presence of water.

Traditional landscapes contain six elements: rocks, trees, waterfalls, rivers, people and buildings.

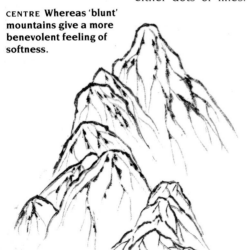

ROCKS

According to Taoist principles, rocks have three faces and there are fascinating names to describe the strokes used to illustrate them. Lotus vein is shown in the above examples, other names include ravelled hemp, ax cuts, and iron bands. Modelling strokes often interlink the structure of the mountains giving each range a unity of style since geology, in Chinese Brush Painting changes little.

The strokes used should be lively and to achieve this the brush should 'dance' across the paper. Keep your wrist very flexible and move the brush from upright to oblique position and back again. Do not paint the mountains as a dominant outline filled in with a few pale strokes – the modelling strokes should all be part of the structure of the rocks.

TREES

Many landscapes feature trees, either in the foreground or in the distance. One suggested guideline is that a tree should have four main branches. Another is that trees are frequently found in groups, one supporting another. Your landscape will appear realistic if the trees look natural both in their setting and attitude. Do not feel that you have to paint foliage on all trees – one or two may have died. Be sure not to include varieties that do not grow in the particular climate you have chosen.

Most people find it easier to start painting the tree from the base so the strokes become lighter as you progress up the tree. There are artists who start at the outer edge of the tree and work inwards, but a clear 'picture' is required in the mind in order to do this.

A few foliage shapes are shown here, and many more are featured in other books especially *The Mustard Seed Garden Manual of Painting* – a facsimile of a very ancient book. In all paintings you should be aware of scale, and this is especially relevant in positioning trees in landscapes. More detail can be used if the tree is large, less if it is shown in the distance.

Trees can feature in figure and bird paintings as well as landscapes. They may form a major part of the work or merely be an accessory.

BELOW These tree trunk examples show varying shapes and attitudes. Note the differing scale and proximity of the different examples. Distance will always lend an air of mystery to the composition, especially if there are trees or outcrops of rock to suggest something hidden.

LEFT Leaf shapes and groupings can be varied according to the varieties of trees, the terrain and geographical area being depicted. Comparative scales however should be observed so the trees do not appear too large or too small compared with their neighbours.

97

LANDSCAPE FAN

This landscape has been painted on a fan. The trees were painted in shades of black, together with the rocks in the foreground, and light grey was used for the distant mountains. The foreground was painted first so the colours could gradually become lighter to give the impression of distance.

Fans are available ready folded and mounted, so that no paper mounting is necessary. The bamboo framework is purchased separately. The paper area is rather like a semi-meticulous paper and will take lines very well although it needs care against smudging. Once the design has been completed, the sticks can be slid into position and the cover sticks pasted to each end. With care this will give a well-finished article.

3 **ABOVE** Add additional detail and modelling until you have sufficient objects of interest in the painting.

1 **ABOVE** First paint the outline of the trees in the foreground, together with the rocks. Fan paper is very similar to meticulous, and will allow fine lines.

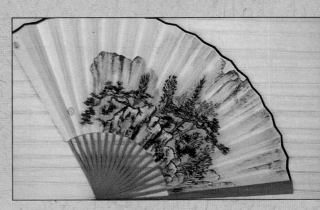

4 **ABOVE** This is the completed fan, after the sticks have been inserted into the pockets and the end covers glued into place. The fan can be used for its original purpose, hung on the wall, or propped up on a small stand for display.

2 **LEFT** Colour the foreground and background with a light colour to suit mood of the picture. Do not use colours or shades for the background which conflict with the foreground, as you should try to give depth to the painting. A feeling of depth will be achieved by using different shades of the same colour or similar colours, with the lighter colour for the background objects.

4

BELOW A detail of the
completed fan. The fan
shape may pose certain
problems for the
inexperienced painter
but the results are
worth the effort.

SIMPLE LANDSCAPES

The three examples illustrate some techniques and show easy variations in composition. The first one suggests two waterfalls, the second a gorge with plenty of room for birds to fly and the third has even more misty space and some trees.

   The paints can be burnt sienna and sky blue, the traditional landscape colours, used lightly. A darker blue such as indigo can be used very faintly on the distant mountains as it was in the past. Any colour on the trees should be light.

   The colouring of a landscape can be painted as strokes or by the wash technique discussed earlier. In this case, dampen the paper all over but select the areas for the coloured wash with care so that the misty areas have softer edges.

1 **TOP LEFT** The stages are shown as three different compositions to give more examples. Start the landscape by using grey ink and paint the foreground and the distance. In other words the frame of the picture. Leave space in between where you intend to paint the focal subject of the picture. Waterfalls and gorges can be included at this stage.

2 **BOTTOM LEFT** Add the darker, foreground details, making sure that you add to the whole area of rock, not just the outline. One of the secrets of landscape work is to avoid completely outlining anything. Ensure that your lines have breaks in them, that solid, dry and outline strokes are all used to add interest. The modelling strokes should be part of the rocks rather than separate.

3 **BELOW RIGHT** The completed landscape. Remember, ink and light colour are frequently used. The tree on the right is illustrated with dots and the pine tree with small groups of lines forming the needle shapes. Place the side of the brush down for the pine tree colouring.

LEFT Willow trees are a favourite subject of Chinese Brush painters, perhaps because the fountain-like fall of the branches evokes a feeling of serene calm. It is therefore important to get the attitude of the tree correct. This could be used in conjunction with some ducks (painted to a suitable scale).

FIGURES AND BUILDINGS

LEFT This detail from a scroll by Li Geng shows how atmospheric, misty space can be created. The style is distincitve and includes 'ink and light colour' – burnt sienna and sky blue – the traditional landscape colours. This was painted in the year of Ji Wei (could be 1919 or 1979).

**RIGHT The space
between the
foreground and the
mountains is often left
as 'misty' space. This
increases the sense of
enormity of nature and
the distances involved.
The use of washes
heightens the
atmospheric character
of the landscape.
These washes are
carried out in the same
method described for
the fish, except that
they do not cover the
whole of the paper (you
will need to dampen
the complete sheet
however) and they are
painted on the reverse.**

Figures add scale and interest to a painting, showing the insignificance of man against the enormous beauty of nature. As described in the previous chapter, figures require movement and incorporation within the scene.

Buildings are often shown nestling among the trees and rocks, sometimes with scholars or hermits in them.

WATERFALLS AND RIVERS

These often feature in Chinese landscapes, but are generally hinted at rather than shown in detail. As with other subjects, there is no need to show water if a boat is obviously travelling down the river. Similarly once the top of a waterfall has been shown it can disappear into the mists below.

**RIGHT This detail
of a landscape in
traditional style shows
a combination of many
modelling strokes. It is
a copy, painted in 1980,
of an earlier work by
Lan Tao in the 17th
century.**

**FAR RIGHT This detail
from the Lan Tao copy is
painted in outline style
with colour added to
give it solidarity. The
building on stilts is
typical of many Chinese
landscapes as are the
figures shown
discussing their daily
business. Many Chinese
officials retired to the
countryside and spent
hours discussing
painting and poetry.
The crease across the
scroll is partly poor
handling, but it has also
occurred where there is
a joint in the backing
paper. For large
scrolls, the only way to
cover the reverse side
is to piece the backing
paper with overlapping
joints.**

RIGHT **This contemporary landscape by Dai Ying illustrates the running-ink technique – colour and/or water is applied to wet ink. This forces the ink and colour to run into the paper. This method of painting is further dealt with in the final chapter**

LEFT **This dramatic and effective modern painting showing a lotus pond in moonlight was painted by Bo Yun who lives and paints in China. The lotus flowers are probably in gouache as they are very opaque.**

THE FINISHED
PICTURE

SEALS AND
CALLIGRAPHY

The Chinese say that no painting is complete without calligraphy and a seal. This calligraphy can be a poem, a saying, a dedication or simply a signature. You should not spoil your painting with poor calligraphy – yet how can you learn without including it? It is better left until you have practised for quite a while. Beware of what you copy from other paintings – it could be a poem or it may be a political statement!

Another way to sign your paintings is to have your own seal or *chop*. This can be a home-made one carved from a piece of rubber, or one of the beautiful stone varieties carved for you by a seal-carver. To the Chinese, an artist is also a seal-carver, calligrapher and poet.

The text carved onto a seal is often not a name but a saying or part of a poem. The choice of these is endless, although there are some traditional ones. It is possible to order a seal from a Chinese art shop, a specialist society or from abroad. Any translation of names is generally carried out phonetically and, if done properly, is related to the person concerned. The calligraphy for your name can be written in different styles; again this can be ordered from specialists.

There are some ready-made seals such as 'double happiness', 'congratulations' or 'long life'. These are useful for paintings given as presents and are usually inexpensive.

To use the seals, you will need a pile of papers or books (a table surface is too hard) and a pot of red cinnabar paste. This is mercuric sulphide and should be treated with respect as it is poisonous. Having pushed the seal into the paste, making sure that the surface is evenly covered, lower it carefully onto the paper. Make sure the seal is the correct way up. If there is calligraphy carved onto

RIGHT This beautiful calligraphy illustration is by Professor Joseph Lo of 'Seven Brush Strokes Studio' (author's studio name). Professor Lo is a Chinese artist and linguist who has lived in England for many years. Calligraphy means 'beautiful writing' and as Chinese Brush Painting and calligraphy both use the same strokes, a painting is described as being 'written'.

純如玉出於泥舉強叶焰高風小三細節漫花莖
筆下花香如家珍 一九九〇年秋 波林

純如玉出於泥舉強叶臨高風
小三細节漫花莖笔下花香如家珍一九九年秋波林

舉強口於高風
小三細節漫花莖
筆下花香如
家珍一九九年
波林

the side of the seal it should face left. If there is an animal carved on the top, the head should face towards you. Lift the seal away from the paper with care, and try not to smudge the paste. Wipe the seal and your fingers carefully as the paste is very invasive and marks on paper or clothes cannot be removed! The bright red of the seal will enhance your work and make it look more authentic.

The position of the seal is important. To the Western eye it is tempting to fill a blank space, but the seal should always be part of the painting and not destroy or cut across any space. Look at paintings by Chinese artists in galleries or books, and see where the seals are placed. Don't however forget that in books, the empty space is often reduced to fit pictures in with the text, so the top or sides of the work may be cropped and therefore

the spacial concept of the painting diminished for the viewer.

In the past, many seals were impressed onto paintings, often spoiling the original image. From the 12th century onwards, up to fifty seals can be seen on well-illustrated scrolls. Perhaps a painting started out with the artist's seal(s), was given to or purchased by the Emperor, who then included his seal(s). His court were asked for their opinions and these were added as colophons together with more seals! The first seal was used in AD 622, and since then seals have become works of art in their own right. They are carved in either yin or yang (intaglio or relief), or a mixture of the two.

Having completed your painting, added some appropriate calligraphy and one or two seals, you are ready for the final stages.

The kindhearted live a long life.

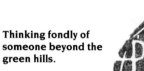

Thinking fondly of someone beyond the green hills.

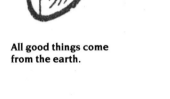

All good things come from the earth.

Flower Monarch

Do not envy glory and profit.

In great peace there is much joy.

Enjoy a little leisure from a busy life.

Warm heat, cold face, proud but calm.

Seals are generally only used in Chinese Brush Painting. However, they may form a logo for a society or company or they may be used as an official stamp on a document. These seals were carved from various rock formations by Qu Lei Lei.

Cherish the memory of you 12 hours a day.

An intimate friend at a remote corner of the world.

Plant plum trees thinly with a plough on clear days.

Fame

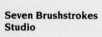

Seven Brushstrokes Studio

Long Life

Year of the Sheep

LEFT Tiny seals made of jade are useful in illustrating small cards and paintings.

FIXATIVE

At the moment you have a flimsy piece of paper which may be wrinkled if you have used a lot of liquid for your strokes. The Chinese use a pasting process which brings the colours to life and sets the ink and cinnabar giving a more substantial product which can be framed or made into a scroll.

You will need a cold-water starch paste such as wallpaper paste made up slightly thicker than the instructions. The Chinese use wheatstarch flour and water heated together to 80°F, with a few drops of formaldehyde. You will also need a wide dry brush to remove wrinkles from the paper, one wide and one small pasting brush, a spray bottle filled with clean water, a drinking straw, silicone polish, newspaper, a couple of damp cloths, a dry duster, a piece of dowel or tube longer than the width of your painting, and a piece of the same or similar paper to that used for the painting approximately 50mm larger on all sides. The work surface can be a formica table, enamelled surface or similar. You will also need a piece of blockboard, plywood or hardboard (if the painting is small) to paste the painting onto while it dries. You can also use a painted or veneered door which has been varnished. The process will not mark the door as the paste is water-based and can be removed with a damp cloth.

Using the polish, you should make sure the work surface is clean and slippery. This enables the painting to slide easily. Place the painting face-down and lightly spray the back with water. Using the dry brush, gently smooth out any wrinkles working from the centre outwards. Carefully roll up the painting and set to one side. Wipe the table. Place the backing paper, smooth side up on the table, having checked that there are no hairs or spots on it. Again working out from the centre, paste evenly but do not be too concerned about any wrinkles. Lift the pasted sheet by the corners and put it down to one side on a dry sheet of newspaper with the paste uppermost. Wipe out the paste brush and go over the pasted sheet to push as much water as possible into the newspaper (but do not be too heavy handed). Having cleaned the paste from the table, wipe over with a dry cloth, then lay the painting face-down again, and if necessary, brush with the dry brush. Lift the pasted

paper with one end wrapped around the dowel to support it and make it easier to hold with one hand. Check for hairs and bits! Lower the opposite end gently onto the painting leaving a margin of 50mm. Use the dry brush gently to brush out any wrinkles as you lower the pasted paper. If it goes down badly, lift it off again and reposition. It is possible, even after the paste is dry, to separate the two pieces of paper by soaking, provided a reasonable quality of paper has been used. Gradually increase the pressure when brushing to ensure that the two pieces of paper are bonded together. With the small paste brush, paste around the excess paper. Tear off two small pieces of newspaper and fold in half. Place this folded paper on two corners of the pasted paper to strengthen the lifting points. Lift the finished product off the table and attach it to the door or vertical board with the painting facing out. Locate the top of the sheet first, then the sides, followed by the base. Make sure that the edges are attached to the door surface all round. Insert the straw and gently blow some air underneath. Leave at least overnight to dry thoroughly.

If the colour starts to run (there is less risk with this method as the painting itself is not pasted), wet the offending spot thoroughly with a cloth and blot with clean tissue. When applying the tissue a second or third time make sure it is clean or the colour will spread further. The reason for the colour running is most likely to be excessive or unsuitable pigment.

When dry, the painting should be very flat similar to watercolour paper that has been stretched. With a round bladed knife, ease it from the door and trim to size. The whole process can be repeated as many times as you like to obtain a thicker backing. If making a scroll however, you only need to back with a single sheet.

Alternatively, you can paste the back of the painting with care, removing all wrinkles, and then lower a sheet of thin board onto it (not card as this is made in layers and will separate). After brushing to ensure that all air bubbles are removed, lift the painting carefully and leave face-up to dry, before trimming. This method is more risky if you use Western watercolours, and the dry sheet, although it is more substantial, will need to be put under books or weights to flatten for a week. Make sure it is completely dry otherwise mould may grow on the painting.

MOUNTING

The next stage is to put a card or silk brocade mount around the painting. The latter can be done by specialists and some framing shops. The size of the area around your painting is a matter of personal preference. Oriental proportions are: the width of the painting above (Heaven), two thirds of the width of the painting below (earth), and a sixth of the width of the painting to each side (showing that you are capturing a moment in time). In the West, people often prefer either the scroll format or equal space all round.

Frames can be of wood or metal. Simple frames will show the pictures to their best advantage: ornate frames may be too distracting. Scroll-making is a specialist subject and probably best left to the experts. This will be more expensive than framing, especially as silk has continually increased in price. It is also a process that cannot be hurried.

LEFT **This beautiful old hanging scroll by Wang Yu in ink and colour is from an exhibition held in 1990 entitled 'Escape from the Dusty World', reproduced by kind permission of the Sydney L Moss Gallery, London.**

SOURCES OF INSPIRATION

BELOW This experimental landscape by the author was inspired by a photograph of the Li River and reflects the words of the poem, 'I escape to the mountains along the flow of ink'. The reflection was achieved by making the hills very wet and then folding the paper in half. You should be careful not to create handprints when pressing the lower half of the paper onto the painted surface.

Your eventual aim should be to paint your own subjects without reference to anyone else's version. The Chinese feel very strongly about fraud, and if they use another's painting as a guide, they will say 'in the style of'. This is one important reason for signing or putting your seal on your work, especially as in the West we attach great value to originality. Even Masters whose paintings are exhibited by museums include some appropriate calligraphy on their paintings if the work is not their own inspiration. Obviously, if you are taught by

someone how to paint fish for example, your work is likely to have the 'flavour' of that person, even when you no longer use their work as inspiration. If you have several tutors your work is likely to be an amalgam of their styles, and you will select what appeals to you most – this is certainly so in my case. The Chinese say that even in copying you will always put something of yourself into the painting – you would therefore have to subdue 'self' to carry out a perfect copy.

With practice you may find that you can visualize most of the painting but need a reference

LEFT **This painting was also again inspired from a photograph. Qutang Gorge is a dramatic scene and as Yuan shu paper is so yellow, white has had to be added to achieve the mist effect.**

for a small part of it which could come from previous work, illustrations in books and magazines, or exhibition catalogues etc. The goldfish in Chapter 9 for instance were influenced by a technique shown by Sheena Davis and Jane Evans. It is a way of painting that subject rather than a direct copy.

Exposure to other artists' work is very important, especially if you are observant and critical. Decide what you like about a painting, also what you do not like. Look at how they have 'managed' the white paper, where the spaces are and their importance within the whole composition. Try a painting similar to the one in front of you, then change the composition or form to suit your taste. When finished you should look at both and ask yourself if you have made an improvement.

Look at both old and new work. Techniques that perhaps do not appeal at first may turn out to suit you very well. As in all art forms, there are many different styles, far more than are mentioned in this book, and beauty is in the eye of the beholder. You will find that a picture you enjoyed painting will not necessarily be appreciated by others, but your pleasure in carrying out the work is all that matters. A great advantage of Chinese Brush Painting is its speed in comparison with the time required for many Western techniques.

Once you have gained confidence and feel you have mastered the spacial concepts and the minimalist approach, you can branch out on your own and work from sketches, photographs and real life. The traditional way of viewing a subject was to keep all the details in the mind, and often the painting was carried out some considerable time later. Chinese artists seem to 'pull a painting out of the air' because they are so familiar with the main features of their subject. Try to cultivate this close observation. Sketches are a way of deciding on the spot what the main features are. Working from photographs will tempt you to put too much detail into the painting. If you are unable to go to China, then photographs, magazines and films are the best ways to absorb the elements of Chinese life and customs. Of course you do not have to portray Chinese scenes but can use all the techniques to illustrate your own surroundings or favourite places.

ABOVE **This tree frog was inspired by a photograph by Stephen Dalton, published in** *Secret Lives.* **It is painted on mulberry paper. Many books are available with superb photographs, the problem is a temptation to include too much detail. The original background material was not included in this case.**

ADVANCED
TECHNIQUES

Once you have started painting, you will find that certain styles and techniques appeal to you more than others. Whatever gives you pleasure is worth pursuing, even if you are not successful initially. But you should not close your mind to other developments in this exciting art form.

Some Chinese artists living in the West have used a combination of Eastern and Western techniques to explore new possibilities. Even if some methods have a close relation to forms of Western art, the behaviour of the paper and the quality of the brush will always add a new dimension.

RESIST TECHNIQUES

This has an affinity with batik. It is especially useful with suitable calligraphy as shown in the example by Qu Lei Lei. The character is 'snow' and the texture on the paper reinforces this theme.

To achieve this effect splash milk on the paper (the higher the fat content the better), and write the character over the top. Experiment by letting the milk dry before adding the ink strokes, by painting on the other side of the paper to the milk and by varying the ink tones. The ink and strokes should echo the conditions and the subject – wet strokes for a poem about rain, and dry strokes for one extolling the virtues of living in the desert.

Equally effective are thin staggered milk strokes painted diagonally across the painting with the character for rain or fountain. Once you have tried this with calligraphy, use the technique with a landscape or a figure under an umbrella to suggest a rainy scene. Use strokes that are in proportion; it would look wrong to have raindrops like spears!

You can achieve different effects either by putting a wash over the work and splattering with tiny spots of white gouache, or by splashing the gouache on first and then applying the wash. The gouache, being more opaque than Chinese white, will show up more.

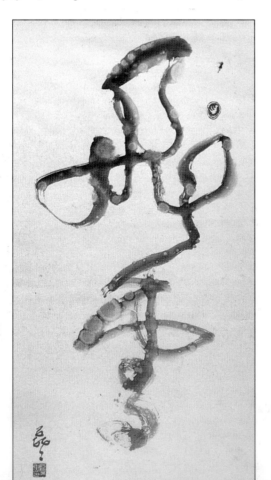

RIGHT **The character for 'snowy' by Qu Lei Lei used with the resist milk technique. This uses the principles of batik to provide a resistance against penetration by the ink.**

FAR RIGHT **Any characters or scenes can be used but the painting will have far more meaning if appropriate subjects are chosen. The author also chose the character for 'snow' to demonstrate the milk technique but preferred to stick to a more standard style.**

114

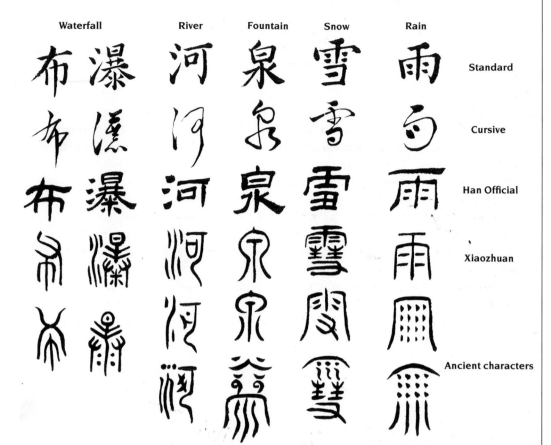

Waterfall	River	Fountain	Snow	Rain	
					Standard
					Cursive
					Han Official
					Xiaozhuan
					Ancient characters

LEFT These calligraphy examples by Qu Lei Lei are all suitable for the milk technique. It is a useful exercise to persuade artists to practice calligraphy and demonstrates the difference between the varying styles.

LEFT This simple landscape demonstrates the use of milk strokes to imitate rain. Avoid using too many lines or spacing them too evenly. Dots of milk could be used to give the effect of snow. These could be sprayed on using a fixative sprayer.

WRINKLING

Wrinkling is used to provide texture. Crush the paper to be used into a ball. Smooth out the paper and gently run a loaded brush over the high points. When the work has been mounted the creases will disappear and the textured lines remain. This technique is often used for trees, both trunks and foliage. It can also be used to increase interest in a fish painting. The fish example shown has been mounted to eliminate the creases. Do not use too dark or too bright a colour for the wash.

A very modern technique inspired by Qu Lei Lei can also be used for trees. This uses a modest amount of wrinkling, and the application of light colours such as stone green on the front of the paper and darker colours, indigo and black, on the back. Putting another colour on the back not only throws the lighter colour into relief but also pushes it back out of the paper. When mounted the colours may run, but this will add to the general effect.

This technique is shown in several stages, involving not only the wrinkle method but also the blotting technique described below. Full use is made of the absorbent qualities of various papers. Experiment with different ones as each will give a different effect.

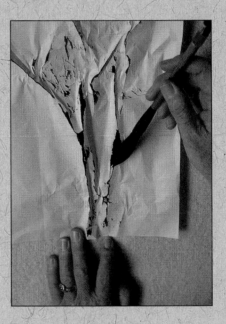

1 **ABOVE** Crease the paper as required using both hands. The amount of detail in the creasing will depend on the scale of the painting and the subject. This technique often benefits from not having too many preconceived ideas and just to 'let it happen'. This is one advantage of an art form which does not use expensive surfaces to paint on.

2 **ABOVE** Run a dry, black brush along the creases to form trees etc. The amount of ink and the depth of colour will depend on the desired effect and individual taste.

3 **ABOVE** Fill in the trunks of the trees with burnt sienna. If the picture is sufficiently large you could also fill in some of the branches.

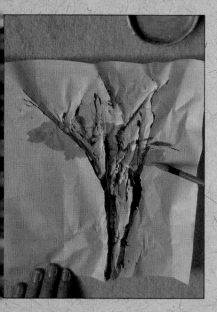

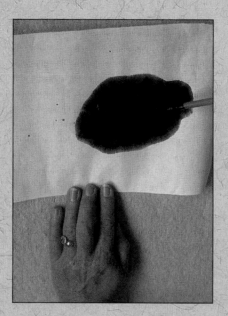

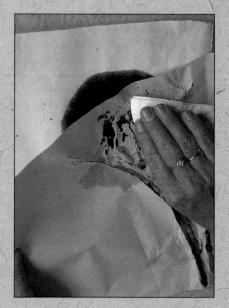

4 **ABOVE** Add light green as required. Both Chinese mineral green or Teppachi light green would be suitable.

6 **ABOVE** Cover a spare piece of paper with black ink. It is important to carry out this stage quickly before the ink has time to soak into the paper too much.

6 **ABOVE** Blot your painting onto the wet ink (beware hand prints!). Again the level of 'darkness' you include depends on the proposed atmosphere.

7 **ABOVE** Add some black or dark blue ink on the back of the painting with a brush, especially behind some of the light green.

8 **ABOVE** Add any dark, dry strokes that you consider necessary to contrast with the rest. You should now have a good look at the painting to see if any figures or other detail need be added. Pin the painting up somewhere and stand back to see it from a distance. This advice applies to all your paintings.

9 ABOVE The completed painting. An atmosphere
of coolness, mystery and dark recesses has
resulted from the various stages. Calligraphy and
seals can be added if desired.

BLOTTING COLOUR

You can transfer colour easily from one piece of paper to another, in fact this often happens when you do not want it to! To achieve the effects in the example by Qu Lei Lei (below), paint the required shape onto a spare piece of paper, place the painting on top and press down evenly, making sure not to transfer handprints as well. With some imagination you can produce some really exciting effects. Try not to set out with a particular theme or result in mind, but play with the paper and paint, hesitating occasionally, even letting the whole lot dry and hanging it up for a few days, before beginning the next stage. If you wish the paint and ink to blend you may need to dampen the painting with clean water before proceeding.

With all these techniques, the Xuan and Yuan shu papers give good results, but practice papers can be used provided more care is taken in handling them as they may disintegrate more easily.

LEFT This painting by Qu Lei Lei on Yuan shu paper is taken from his *English Life* series of paintings and uses a blotting technique on the house and ground. The tree is painted both from in front and behind.

FAR RIGHT **This Spring blossom is painted in the style favoured by Dai Ying. The seal says 'apricot blossoms in the spring rain' and it provided the inspiration for this painting.**

BELOW **Break ink technique – a simple demonstration sheet is used to show students the contrast between wet and dry strokes. Where the various break-ink methods have been used (light-break-dark, dark-break-light, water-break-ink and Ink-break-water) you can see the soft transition between colours of ink that has been created.**

BREAK-INK TECHNIQUES

These techniques have such descriptive and typically Chinese names, such as 'ink-break-water' or 'light-break-dark'. For ink-break-water, clean water is applied to the paper followed by different shades and viscosity of ink and paint. The brush-strokes can be in thick ink or wet ink.

Water-break-ink is not surprisingly the reverse, with water being added after the ink strokes have been made. The ink will extend beyond the original boundaries and try to follow the water. Using this technique on part of the painting rather than all over gives more contrast.

Light-break-dark and dark-break-light speak for themselves, with light ink or paint being applied over parts of dark strokes and vice versa.

Landscapes are perhaps the best subject to try out these techniques. You will learn a lot about the qualities of the paper and ink and get differing effects depending which paper you use. An absorbent paper will give a far more exaggerated effect than semi-absorbent paper. None of these techniques is suitable for sized paper.

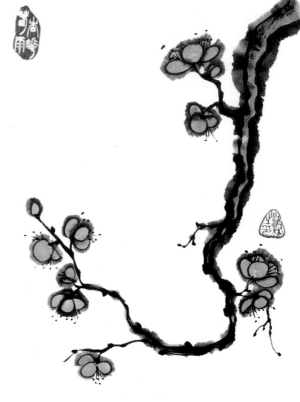

RUNNING INK

There are several examples of work by Dai Ying in this chapter and elsewhere in the book which illustrate the running ink technique. The aim is to use wet ink and to add colour and/or water before the wet ink has dried. This forces the ink and colour to run into the paper.

This method works well on thicker papers where the ink takes longer to dry. It is also effective when colour is placed between two lines or within a flower shape. The ink is then pushed in one direction only and the inner edge of the line remains clean. Controlling the amount of ink and using thick paper will enable you to persuade the ink to travel quite a distance.

To paint the apricot blossom, first mix burnt sienna with water in the palette, followed by light green or pink. Put in the two outline strokes for the branch with black ink. Work quickly and with a brush that is not too small. Immediately run a wet brush of burnt sienna down the centre of the stem. If this is not enough add some water as well. When you feel the ink has travelled far enough blot with a tissue. If the ink does not flow far enough, try using more ink or work in smaller sections.

The flowers are painted individually, again taking care not to use too small a brush or the ink will dry too quickly. In this case add extra water. To provide contrast with the wet technique, the stamens are added last with very black ink, when the colour and ink are dry.

LEFT **These trees, painted using the running-ink technique, are a contemporary shape and will not appeal to everyone. There are many subjects which could be explored using a combination of different techniques and styles.**

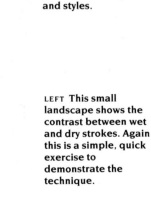

LEFT **This small landscape shows the contrast between wet and dry strokes. Again this is a simple, quick exercise to demonstrate the technique.**

ALTERNATIVE USES
FOR PAINTINGS

BELOW On this set of laminated tablemats, each setting with a different, colour co-ordinated flower, the original artwork has been preserved under the lamination. These are illustrated by kind permission of Mr and Mrs Robin Kraike.

Chinese Brush Painting techniques can be used on almost any absorbent surface – pottery (biscuitware which is glazed after painting), silk or fabric upholstery and clothing (use special washable paints), cards and calendars, fans, small pictures and fabric scrolls. If using underglaze or fabric paints it is best not to use your best brushes; buy a cheaper set to keep for such work. Whatever medium you use, whether watercolour, ink or special paint, you should always wash your brushes out carefully at the end of the session. If really necessary soap can be used occasionally to remove stubborn colour.

CONCLUSION

Of course the first rule of Chinese Brush Painting is to enjoy your painting; let the brush dance across the paper with liveliness and imagination. There are bound to be times when the mood is just not right, and other times when every stroke is a success. Practice is important, but if nothing will work at the time then change the subject or leave it for a while. Some find that they work better when sad, others when they are happy. Through this art form, many friendships have been made, and talents discovered – may it be the same for you.

ABOVE **This bird detail from a painting by Dai Ying uses a very wet technique on thick Xuan paper. Extra colour and water is added to 'push' the ink through and along the paper before the ink has dried.**

LEFT **This detail of** *Crane* **in running-ink style is made all the more interesting by the contrast of the graceful bird shape and the rhythm of the reeds.**

SUPPLIERS

Many art shops sell individual items but are often unsure if stock is Chinese or Japanese. Several kits are now available by firms such as Osmiroid and Inscribe and often include an instruction book. Specialist or regular suppliers are listed in alphabetical order below.

The Chinese Brush Painters Society caters for those interested in Chinese Paintings. Apply to the Secretary, Carpenters Seven, Grange Road, Alresford, Hampshire SO24 9HE, UK.

UK

Arts and Graphics, 21 West End, Redruth, Cornwall

Bamboo Grove, York

Chinese Art Centre, 50 High Street, Oxford, OX1 4AS

Chinese Arts Gallery, Ambleside, Cumbria, LA22 0BZ

Collets Chinese Bookshop, 40 Great Russell Street, London, WC1B 3PJ (*mainly books*)

Deben Gallery, 26 Market Hill, Woodbridge, Suffolk, IP12 4LU

Falkiner Fine Papers, 117 Long Acre, London, WC2E 9PA

Frank Herring, 27 High West Street, Dorchester, Dorset

Gough Bros, Bognor Regis

Greyfriars Art Shop, 1 Greyfriars Place, Edinburgh

Guanghwa Co, 7–9 Newport Place, London WC2H 7JR

Guangming Co, 22 Berry Street, Liverpool

Harberton Art Workshop, 27 High Street, Totnes, Devon, TQ9 5NP

Jennifer Scott, Coach Hill House, Burley Street, Ringwood, Hants BH24 4HN (*mail order or callers by arrangement*)

Kam Cheung, 28–30 Burleigh Street, Cambridge, CB1 1DG

M & R Chinese Arts, 309–310 Bull Ring, Birmingham

Neal Street East, 5–7 Neal Street, Covent Garden, London, WC2H 9PU

Samarkand Gifts, 31–35 Elm Hill, Norwich

Typhoon Ltd, 64 Long Acre, Covent Garden, London, WC2E 9JH

Wagen Arts, Hemel Hempstead, Herts

Ying Hwa Co Ltd, 14 Gerrard Street, London, W1

USA

Arthur Brown & Bros, 2 West 46th Street, New York, NY 10036

China Art Materials, China Cultural Centre, 970 North Broadway Suite 210, Los Angeles, CA 90012

Chinese Culture Co, 736–738 7th Street NW, Washington, DC 20001

Chinese Culture Co, 126 N 10th Street, Philadelphia, PA 19107

Chinese Culture Co, 843 Clement Street, San Francisco, CA 94118

Co-op Artists Materials, PO Box 53097, Atlanta, GA 30355

Daniel Smith Inc, 4130 First Avenue S, Seattle, WA 98134

Denver Art Supply, 1437 California Street, Denver, CO 80202

Harvard Square Art Centre, 17 Holyoke Street, Cambridge, MA 02138

Oriental Culture Enterprises, 22 Pell Street, New York, NY 10013

Pearl Art & Craft Supplies, 5695 Telegraph Road, Alexandria, VA 22303

Unique Artists Supply Co, 838 Grant Avenue, San Francisco, CA 94108

Utrecht Art Centre, 332 South Michigan, Chicago, IL 60604

AUSTRALIA

Artery, 31 Davey Street, Hobart 7000

Artist Supply Co, 83 George Street, Sydney 2000

Art Paper and Supplies, 243 Sterling Highway, Claremont 6010

Art Requirements, 1 Dickson Street, Wooloowin 4030

David Wang Emporium, 152 Bourke Street, Melbourne 3000

Eckersleys, 55 Elizabeth Street, Melbourne 3000

Eckersleys, 21 Frome Street, Adelaide 5000

Eckersleys, 116 Commercial Road, Prahran, Victoria 3181

Jackson's, 148 William Street, Perth 6000

Oxford Art Supplies, 221 Oxford Street, Darlinghurst 2010

Oxlades Art Centre, 136 Wickham Street, Fortitude Valley, Queensland 4006

Philip Craft Supplies, 53 Cobee Court, Philip 2606

CREDITS

Photography for brush holding and wrinkling technique – David Cherrett, *Crane* by Fu Hua – Catherine Rees Jones, *Landscape* by Wang Yu and *Album Leaf* – Sydney L Moss Gallery.

Thanks to all artists for permission to include their work and to the Sydney L Moss Gallery for their photographs. Grateful thanks go to all who have given help and encouragement, especially Dave, Barbara, Margaret, Tess, Brian and Lei Lei. Also to Sally Harper and Sarah Buckley.

Attempts to contact Pu Chuan, and Li Geng for permission to feature scrolls owned by the author have been unsuccessful.

INDEX

Page references in italics refer to illustrations and/or their captions.